John Creasor

Revised by laws of the township of Derby in the county of Grey

John Creasor

Revised by laws of the township of Derby in the county of Grey

ISBN/EAN: 9783741184406

Manufactured in Europe, USA, Canada, Australia, Japa

Cover: Foto ©Lupo / pixelio.de

Manufactured and distributed by brebook publishing software
(www.brebook.com)

John Creasor

Revised by laws of the township of Derby in the county of Grey

REVISED BY-LAWS

—OF THE—

TOWNSHIP OF DERBY,

IN THE COUNTY OF GREY.

REVIEWED AND CORRECTED BY

MR. JOHN CREASOR, Q.C.

Of the Law Firm of Messrs. Creasor & Morrison, Owen Sound.

ALSO, STATUTORY ACTS RESPECTING LINE FENCES, DITCHES
. AND WATER COURSES, NOXIOUS WEEDS, HEALTH, &c.

JOHN ROBERTSON, ESQ., · REEVE.

OWEN SOUND

JNO. RUTHERFORD, STEAM BOOK AND JOB PRINTER.

1886.

TABLE OF CONTENTS.

PREFACE.

The Council of 1885, realizing the necessity of having the standing By-laws of the Township revised and printed, appointed the Reeve and Clerk to take charge of the matter, and authorized them to have such By-laws as might be the subjects of litigation in their operation submitted to a legal adviser. In pursuance of this they choose the firm of Messrs. Creasor & Morrison, Owen Sound, and the work of reviewing and correcting was performed by Mr. John Creasor, Q.C., the senior member of the firm.

Mr. Creasor took a deep interest in the work, and in order to produce a model code, undertook to read the proof as they were passing through the press. The work of selecting and preparing a code that would meet the requirements of the ratepayers generally, entailed much more labor and research than was at first anticipated. The chief aim of the Committee and Council was to have the By-laws framed in a plain and practical manner, and in harmony with the authority under which they were made, believing that the information conveyed to the officers and ratepayers through them will tend to prevent rather than encourage litigation.

The Council had some hesitation in passing the By-law imposing a tax on Dogs, &c., and gave the matter a great deal of consideration before doing so. They finally concluded that it was for the interest of the rate-payers generally, as it tended to lessen the number of useless and in some cases dangerous curs, and to encourage the raising of a better class of Dogs ; and also afforded a measure of protection to those who might have the misfortune of suffering through their ravages ; and as the taxes would go into the general funds, they considered that the ratepayers, on an average, would just have to pay so much less on their regular rates.

The Statute Labor By-law received a good deal of attention. The Council intend to use all reasonable means to enforce the faithful perform-ance of Statute Labor, believing that exacting the full amount of labor in each case will tend to the rapid improvement of the roads, and as a conse-quence to a material reduction in the taxes.

The attention of Overseers of Highways, and the ratepayers generally, is specially called to the observance of the By-laws with respect to obstruc-tions on the Highways and the removal of Fences where found enclosing any portion of the road allowance. The Council feel it to be their imperative duty to exact a strict compliance with the law in these respects, and hope that it will be observed without having to resort to compulsory measures.

Persons appointed to office are hereby reminded that they cannot legally enforce their authority until they have made the declaration of office ; and as the law makes this an imperative duty, it is hoped that none will run the risk of neglecting its observance.

Whatever the Committee may have lacked in ability they feel that they cannot be charged with a lack of desire to perform the duty entrusted to them faithfully, with the best interests of the ratepayers and the credit of the Township constantly in view.

All of which is respectfully submitted.

> JOHN ROBERTSON, Reeve.
> W. BEATON, Township Clerk,

Derby, Feb. 1886.

BY-LAWS.

BY-LAW No. 3 of 1886,

To establish Standing Rules and Regulations for the guidance of the Council of the Corporation of the Township of Derby, in the County of Grey, in the transaction of business.

Whereas it is desirable to adopt and define Standing Rules to regulate and govern the proceedings of the Council :

Be it therefore enacted by the Municipal Council of the Corporation of the Township of Derby, in the County of Grey, as follows :

1. The members of Council shall hold their first meeting in each year on the day and hour appointed by Statute, and all subsequent meetings shall be held monthly on the first Saturday in each month thereafter, at 10 o'clock in the forenoon.

2. The Reeve shall have power to call a special meeting of Council at any time that he may consider it expedient for the interest of the Municipality ; but no grants of money shall be made, or pecuniary liability incurred at such special meeting, unless the same shall be referred to in the notice calling the meeting.

3. A majority of the whole number of members required by law to constitute the Council shall be necessary to form a quorum.

4. At the first meeting of the new Council in each year, after the duties required by Statute are completed, the following standing committees for the then current year shall be chosen for looking after the business pertaining to their respective committees

(1.) Road and Bridge Committee, to be composed of all the members of Council.

(2.) Assessment and Collector's Roll Committee, to be composed of two members.

(3.) Finance Committee, to be composed of two members.

5. The first person named shall be chairman and convener of the Committee on which he is chosen.

6. It shall be the duty of the Road and Bridge Committee at all seasons of the year to have the general oversight of the Township Roads and Bridges ; and shall have power in cases of Bridges, Culverts, and other pieces of roads, being suddenly rendered dangerous by freshets or otherwise, to have them repaired forthwith ; provided the expenditure does not exceed ten dollars ; otherwise it will be their duty to ask the Reeve to call a special meeting of Council to consider the matter, if they deem it unsafe for the public travel to have it left over until the next regular meeting.

It shall also be their duty to report on the propriety of making grants to applicants, or otherwise, in pursuance of the By-law with respect to wire fences in certain localities for the benefit of the roads in winter ; and also with respect to purchasing gravel and gravel pits, and all other matters pertaining to the improvement of roads.

It shall also be their duty to submit a report at the May meeting of Council, embracing the following particulars :

(1.) The general condition of Roads all over the Township, as far as they have been able to ascertain.

(2.) Pieces of Roads for which application has been made to them, and requiring special attention.

(3.) An estimate of the amount that they deem advisable to expend on the roads during the season. And the said report, as passed in Committee of the whole Council, shall be made as nearly as practicable the basis of expenditure on the roads during the remainder of the season.

7. It shall be the duty of the Assessment and Collectors' Roll Committee :

(1.) To enquire into the fitness and capability by education and otherwise, of applicants for the offices of Assessor and Collector respectively.

(2.) To meet in the Clerk's office previous to the Court of Revision in each year, to examine and report on the condition of the Assessment Roll.

(3.) To examine the Collectors' Roll and bond before the Roll is handed over to the Collector.

8. It shall be the duty of the Finance Committee :

(1.) To enquire into the sufficiency of the Treasurer's and Collector's sureties.

(2.) To examine all accounts presented for payment at the Council Board.

(3.) To suggest ways and means of providing funds when necessary.

(4.) To assist the Clerk in preparing the estimates, for levying the rates, and generally to perform all the duties expected of a Finance Committee.

9. The Reeve, or in his absence, the Deputy-Reeve shall preside at the meetings of Council, and shall preserve order and decorum, and decide questions of order.

10. In the absence of both the Reeve and Deputy-Reeve a chairman chosen by the Council shall preside during such absence, and shall, while in the chair, have vested in him all the powers of the Reeve and Deputy.

11. The Reeve shall be ex-officio a member of all committees.

12. Each Committee shall report to the Council on all matters referred to it ; and shall properly number and endorse its reports in the order of their presentation ; and no report shall be presented as the report of a Committee ; which shall not have been approved of at a meeting of the Committee, nor shall the report of a Committee be final or anything done by virtue thereof, until such report is approved by the Council.

13. In all matters of procedure not provided for by the Municipal Act or these Rules, the rules suggested by the writer of the " Municipal

Councillors' Hand Book," (page 68) shall be followed ; and in all questions as to " Rules of Order," the decision of the Reeve shall be acquiesced in without debate.

JOHN ROBERTSON, REEVE.
W. BEATON, CLERK.

Passed 6th February, 1886.

BY-LAW No. 4 OF 1886.

Relative to Public Morals.

Be it enacted by the Corporation of the Township of Derby, in the County of Grey, as follows : —

1. It shall be unlawful for any person or persons to sell or give any intoxicating drink to a child, apprentice, or servant, within the Township of Derby, without the consent of a parent, master, or legal protector.

2. It shall be unlawful for any person or persons to post indecent placards, writings, or pictures, or to write indecent words, or make indecent pictures or drawings on the walls or fences in streets or public places within the Township of Derby ; nor shall any person exhibit, sell, or offer to sell any indecent or lewd book, paper, picture, plate, drawing or other thing, or exhibit, or perform any indecent, immoral, or lewd play within the said Township.

3. It shall be unlawful for any person or persons within the Township of Derby to use indecent, obscene, or profane language, or to address to any person in public, any indecent, offensive or insulting language.

4. Vice, drunkenness, profane swearing, obscene, blasphemous, or grossly insulting language and other immorality and indecency are hereby prohibited, and declared to be unlawful in the Township of Derby.

5. It shall be unlawful for any person or persons to keep a disorderly house or a house of ill-fame within the Township of Derby.

6. It shall be unlawful for any person or persons to keep a gambling house in the Township of Derby ; and any constable or or other peace officer having jurisdiction in the Township of Derby aforesaid, may at any time enter any gambling house and seize and destroy any faro banks, rouge-et-noir, roulettee tables, or other devices for gambling found therein.

7. Indecent public exposure of the person and other indecent exhibitions are hereby prohibited and declared to be unlawful in the Township of Derby.

8. Any person or persons guilty of an infraction of any of the provisions of this By-law, shall upon conviction before any Justice or Justices of the Peace, on the oath or affirmation of any credible witness, forfeit and pay, at the discretion of the said Justice or Justices convicting, a penalty not exceeding the sum of Fifty Dollars for each offence, exclusive of costs ; and in default of payment thereof forthwith, it shall and may be lawful for the Justice convicting as aforesaid, to issue a warrant under his hand and seal ; or in case any two Justices are acting together therein, then under the hand and seal of one of

them, to levy the said penalty and costs, or costs only, by distress and sale of the goods and chattels of the offender or offenders ; and in case of no sufficient distress to satisfy the said penalty and costs, it shall and may be lawful for the Justice aforesaid to commit the offender or offenders to the Common Gaol of the County of Grey, with or without hard labor, for any period not exceeding twenty-one days, unless the said penalty and costs, including costs of committal, be sooner paid.

9. All By-laws, or parts of By-laws of this Corporation which are contrary to or inconsistent with the provisions of this By-law, shall be and the same are hereby repealed.

JOHN ROBERTSON, REEVE.
W. BEATON, CLERK.

Passed 6th Feb., 1886.

BY-LAW No. 5 OF 1886.

By-law respecting Pounds and duties of Pound-keepers and for other purposes.

The Council of the Corporation of the Township of Derby, in the County of Grey, enacts as follows :

1. That every Pound-keeper appointed in the Township of Derby shall, within twenty days after his appointment, make and subscribe the declaration of office according to law.

2. The Corporation of the Township of Derby may provide sufficient yards and enclosures for the safe keep of such animals as it may be the duty of the Pound-keeper to impound.

3. The Revised Statute of Ontario, Chapter 195, shall be in force, except so far as varied by this by-law.

4. The owner of any animal not allowed by this by-law to run at large in the Township of Derby, shall be liable for damages committed by such animal, although the fence enclosing the premises be not of lawful height, or proper construction.

5. That a lawful fence, if of rails, shall be four and a half feet in height, staked and single ridered, or four feet staked and double ridered, or five feet if locked at the angles or along the centre, and in all cases the spaces between the three bottom courses not to be more than five inches apart. Post and board, stone, picket, and wire fences shall be four and a half feet in height ; the spaces between the first two courses of boards not to be more than six inches, and the spaces between the pickets not to be more than three inches. In cases of wire fences, the first twelve inches from the ground to be of board, stone, or other suitable material, and the spaces between the first two strands not to be more than six inches apart, and to be finished with a top piece of board, pole, or scantling, so as to prevent animals from running against it unawares. Lawful division line fences shall be the same as the foregoing, and the sufficiency of the material and construction of the above described fences, or of any other kind not herein described, shall, in cases of dispute, be subject to the decision of the Fence-viewers.

6. It shall not be lawful for any bull, horse, breachy cattle, swine,

sheep, fowls, or poultry, or vicious animals of any kind, to run at large in the Township of Derby ; but other cattle shall be permitted to run at large in the said Township. And any animal running at large contrary to this by-law may be distrained and impounded by any person.

7. That any entire horse, bull, ram, or boar, found running at large in the Township of Derby, shall subject the owner thereof, at the option of the person prosecuting, to the penalty as follows, namely : For entire horse, $8 ; bull, $6 ; ram or boar, $2 ; such penalty may be sued for and collected by complainant before any Justice of the Peace for the County ; or the animal may be impounded, and the Pound-keeper is hereby authorized to take and receive the said penalty in addition to his regular fees. The said penalty to be one moiety to the person prosecuting, and the other moiety to the Township Treasurer, and form part of the general funds.

8. That every fine and penalty imposed by this by-law may be recovered and enforced with costs by a summary proceedings before any Justice of the Peace for the County ; and in default of payment, the offender may be committed to the Common Gaol of the County, there to be imprisoned for any time in the discretion of the convicting and committing Justice not exceeding fourteen days, unless the fine, penalty and costs, including the costs of committal, be sooner paid ; and upon the hearing and trial of any complaint, any person, including the prosecutor, shall be a competent witness, notwithstanding such witness may be entitled to any part of the penalty upon the conviction of the offender. That every penalty recovered under this by-law shall be paid to the Township Treasurer for the use of the Township.

* 9. The fees and charges to be demanded and received under the authority of this by-law shall be as follows, and no more, that is to say :

ANIMALS.	For Impounding.	Food & Water per day.
Horse or Colt	Each 40 cents.	Each 40 cents.
Neat cattle, over 2 years old..	Each 30 "	Each 30 "
Neat cattle, 2 years and under Each	25 "	Each 20 "
Hogs, over 30 lbs. weight....	Each 25 "	Each 25 "
Pigs, 30 lbs. and under.......	Each 10 "	Each 10 "
Sheep :....	Each 10 "	Each 5 "
Poultry or Fowls...........	Each 5 "	Each 5 "

Posting notices, Schedule A, 25c.
Sending notices, Schedule B, 25c.
Sending notices to Fence-Viewers, Schedule D, $1.00
Actual disbursements for postage and advertising in newspapers.

Pound-keepers shall also be entitled to take and receive as commission for selling 2½ per cent. on the proceeds of sale ; and for drawing surety bonds, 20 cents ; to collect and pay to persons distraining and delivering to Pound-keeper each horse or colt, 40 cents ; neat cattle, each 30 cents ; hogs, 20 cents ; sheep, 10 cents ; poultry or fowls, 05 cents ; for delivering notices of distress of strays, 25 cents ; to Fence-viewers for each day attending to examine premises, $2 each ; making and delivering awards, 50 cents.

10. That the Schedules marked A, B, C, D, E, and F, annexed to this by-law, shall form part thereof ; and that the forms of the Schedules, or forms to the like effect, together with the Statute

referred to in section 3 of this by-law, shall be sufficient for the purposes thereof.

11. All by-laws or parts of by-laws of this Corporation, which are contrary to or inconsistent with the provisions of this by-law, shall be and the same are hereby repealed.

JOHN ROBERTSON, REEVE.

W. BEATON, CLERK.

Passed 6th February, 1886.

SCHEDULE REFERRED TO IN THE FOREGOING BY-LAW.

SCHEDULE A.

Notice of Impounding.

Notice is hereby given that on the   day of   last past, at the request of A. B., of this Township, I have impounded certain animals, to wit : (*here give description of animals*) and (*if damages are claimed*) the said A. B. claims the sum of   dollars for damages done on his premises by trespass of said animals. If, therefore, the said animals are not redeemed or replevied, I will sell the same by public auction to the highest bidder, at   at the hour of   o'clock in the (*fore or after*) noon, on the   day of   18

Given under my hand at Derby, this   day of   18

C. D., POUNDKEEPER.

SCHEDULE B.

Notice.

The following animals, viz : (*description*) are impounded (*or distrained*) at lot No.   in the   concession of the Township of Derby, and will there be sold by public auction on the   day of   18   at the hour of   o'clock (*a. m. or p. m.*) if not sooner claimed.

Dated at Derby, this   day of   18

——————, POUNDKEEPER.

SCHEDULE C.

Form of Surety Obligation.

I (*or we*) do hereby bind myself (*or ourselves*) in the sum of (*double value of animals*) dollars, to pay to the owner of the animals impounded at my (*or at request of A. B.*) request this day, all the costs and damages the said owner may suffer by reason of such impounding, if it be decided by law that such impounding was unlawful.

Signed and sealed this   day of   18   , in the presence of

A. B.   { L. S. }
C. D.   { L. S. }

SCHEDULE D.

Notice to Fence-viewers.

To A B, C D, and E F., Fence-viewers of the Township of Derby : Pursuant to by-law of this Township, I do hereby give you notice, and require you and every one of you to attend on the premises of G. H., situate on lot   in the   concession of the Township of Derby, on the   day of   instant, at   o'clock, in the fore (*or after*) noon, then and there to appraise the damages done on said premises, by reason of the trespass of certain animals belonging to J. K., (*or some person unknown*) and determine whether or not the fence enclosing the premises was lawful at the time of trespass.

Given under my hand at Derby, this   day of   18

L. M., POUNDKEEPER.

SCHEDULE E.

Form of Award.

Township of Derby, }
    To Wit : }   We, A B, C D and E F, Fence-viewers of the Township of Derby, having examined the premises and fence enclosing the same of G H., on lot No.   in the   concession of this Township, do hereby award and determine that the fence was (or *was not*) a lawful fence, and adjudge the damages (if any) to be   dollars.

Witness our hands at Derby, this   day of   18

A. B. }
C. D. } FENCE-VIEWERS.
E. F. }

SCHEDULE F.

Statement of demands pursuant to Section 5 of the Statute referred to in Section 3 of this By-law to be made in duplicate.

To A. B., Poundkeeper, at

The following is a statement of my demands against the owner of the animals I have caused to be impounded with you on the   day of   18

1. Delivering (number and description)............... $
2. Damages by reason of trespass of said animals, on
    lot   in the   concession of Derby........ $
3. Poundage fees (when demanded)................... $

In all..................... $.

J. J., DISTRAINER.

In addition to Schedule F, the Pound-keeper may demand a surety obligation in the form of Schedule C.

CHAPTER 195, OF THE REVISED STATUTES OF ONTARIO.

AN ACT RESPECTING POUNDS.

Her Majesty, by and with the advice and consent of the Legislative Assembly of the Province of Ontario, enacts as follows :—

1. Until varied or other provisions are made by by-laws passed under the authority of section four hundred and sixty-three of "*The Municipal Act,*" this Act shall be in force in every Township, City, Town, and incorporated Village in Ontario. 29-30 V. c. 51, s. 355.

2. The owner or occupant of any land shall be responsible for any damage or damages caused by any animal or animals under his charge and keeping, as though such animal or animals were his own property, and the owner of any animal not permitted to run at large by the by-laws of the Municipality shall be liable for any damage done by such animal, though the fence enclosing the premises was not of the height required by such by-laws. 29-30 V. c. 51, s. 355 (1).

3. If not previously replevied, the Pound-keeper shall impound any horse, bull, ox, cow, sheep, goat, pig, or other cattle, geese or any other poultry, distrained for unlawfully running at large, or for trespassing and doing damage, delivered to him for that purpose by any person resident within his division who has distrained the same ; or if the owner of any geese or other poultry refuses or neglects to prevent the same from trespassing on his neighbours' premises after a notice in writing has been served upon him of their trespass, then the owner of such poultry may be brought before any Justice of the Peace and fined such sum as the Justice directs. 29-30 V. c. 51, s. 355 (2).

4. When the common pound of the Municipality or place wherein a distress has been made is not secure, the Poundkeeper may confine the animal in any enclosed place within the limits of the Pound-keeper's division within which the distress was made. 29-30 V. c. 51, s. 355 (3).

5. The owner of any animal impounded shall at any time be entitled to his animal, on demand made therefor, without payment of any poundage fees, on giving satisfactory security to the Pound-keeper for all costs, damages and poundage fees that may be established against him ; but the person distraining and impounding the animal shall, at the time of such impounding, deposit poundage fees, if such are demanded, and within twenty-four hours thereafter deliver to the Pound-keeper duplicate statements in writing of his demands against the owner for damages (if any), not exceeding twenty dollars, done by such animal, exclusive of such poundage fees, and shall also give his written agreement (with a surety if required by the Pound-keeper) in the form following, or in words to the same effect :

"I (*or* we, *as the case may be*) do hereby agree that I (*or* we) will pay to the owner of the (*describing the animal*) by me (A. B.) this day impounded, all costs to which the said owner may be put in case the distress by me the said A. B. proves to be illegal, or in case the claim for damages now put in by me the said A. B. fails to be established." 29-30 V. c. 51, s. 355 (4).

6. In case the animal distrained is a horse, bull, ox, cow, sheep, goat, pig or other cattle, and if the same is distrained by a resident of the Municipality for straying within his premises, such person, instead of delivering the animal to a Pound-keeper, may retain the animal in

his own possession, provided he makes no claim for damages done by the animal, and duly gives the notices hereinafter in that case required of him. 29-30 V. c. 51, s. 355 (5).

7. If the owner is known to him, he shall forthwith give to the owner notice in writing of having taken up the animal. 29-30 V. c. 51, s. 355 (6).

8. If the owner is unknown to the person taking up and retaining possession of the animal, such person shall, within forty-eight hours, deliver to the Clerk of the Municipality a notice in writing of having taken up the animal, and containing a description of the colour, age and natural and artificial marks of the animal, as near as may be. 29-30 V. c. 51, s. 355 (7).

9. The Clerk, on receiving such notice, shall forthwith enter a copy thereof in a book to be kept by him for that purpose, and shall post the notice he receives or copy thereof in some conspicuous place on or near the door of his office, and continue the same so posted for at least one week, unless the animal is sooner claimed by the owner. 29-30 V. c. 51, s. 355 (8).

10. If the animal or any number of animals taken up at the same time is or are of the value of ten dollars or more, the distrainor shall cause a copy of the notice to be published in a newspaper in the County, if one is published therein, and if not, then in a newspaper published in an adjoining County, and to be continued therein once a week for three successive weeks. 29-30 V. c. 51, s. 355 (9).

11. In case an animal is impounded, notices for the sale thereof shall be given by the Pound-keeper or person who impounded the animal within forty-eight hours afterwards, but no pig or poultry shall be sold till after four clear days, nor any horse or other cattle till after eight clear days from the time of impounding the same. 29-30 V. c. 51, s. 355 (10).

12. In case the animal is not impounded, but is retained in the possession of the party distraining the same, if the animal is a pig, goat or sheep, the notices for the sale thereof shall not be given for one month, and if the animal is a horse, or other cattle, the notices shall not be given for two months after the animal is taken up. 29-30 V. c. 51, s. 355 (11).

13. The notices of sale may be written or printed, and shall be affixed and continued for three clear successive days, in three public places in the Municipality, and shall specify the time and place at which the animal will be publicly sold, if not sooner replevied or redeemed by the owner or some one on his behalf, paying the penalty imposed by law (if any) the amount of the injury (if any) claimed or decided to have been committed by the animal to the property of the person who distrained it, together with the lawful fees and charges of the Pound-keeper, and also of the Fence-viewers (if any); and the expense of the animal's keeping. 29-30 V. c. 51, s. 355 (12).

14. Every Pound-keeper, and every person who impounds or confines, or causes to be impounded or confined, any animal in any common pound or in any open or close pound, or in any enclosed place, shall daily furnish the animal with good and sufficient food, water and shelter, during the whole time that such animal continues impounded or confined. 29-30 V. c. 51, s. 355 (13).

15. Every such person who furnishes the animal with food, water and shelter, may recover the value thereof from the owner of the animal, and also a reasonable allowance for his time, trouble and attendance in the premises. 29-30 V. c. 51, s. 355 (14).

16. The value or allowance as aforesaid may be recovered, with costs, by summary proceeding before any Justice of the Peace within whose jurisdiction the animal was impounded, in like manner as fines, penalties or forfeitures for the breach of any by-law of the Municipality may by law be recovered and enforced by a single Justice of the Peace ; and the Justice shall ascertain and determine the amount of such value and allowance when not otherwise fixed by law, adhering, so far as applicable, to the tariff of Pound-keepers' fees and charges established by the by-laws of the Municipality. 29-30 V. c. 51, s. 355 (15).

17. The Pound-keeper, or person so entitled to proceed, may, instead of such summary proceeding, enforce the remuneration to which he is entitled in manner hereinafter mentioned. 29-30 V. c. 51, s. 355 (16).

18. In case it is by affidavit proved before one of the Justices aforesaid, to his satisfaction, that all the proper notices had been duly affixed and published in the manner and for the respective times above prescribed, then if the owner or some one for him does not within the time specified in the notices, or before the sale of the animal, replevy or redeem the same in manner aforesaid, the Pound-keeper who impounded the animal, or if the person who took up the animal did not deliver such animal to any Pound-keeper, but retained the same in his own possession, then any Pound-keeper of the Municipality may publicly sell the animal to the highest bidder, at the time and place mentioned in the aforesaid notices, and after deducting the penalty and the damages (if any) and fees and charges, shall apply the produce in discharge of the value of the food and nourishment, loss of time, trouble and attendance so supplied as aforesaid, and of the expenses of driving or conveying and impounding or confining the animal, and of the sale and attending the same, or incidental thereto, and of the damage when legally claimable (not exceeding twenty dollars,) to be ascertained as aforesaid, done by the animal to the property of the person at whose suit the same was distrained, and shall return the surplus (if any) to the original owner of the animal, or if not claimed by him within three months after the sale, the Pound-keeper shall pay such surplus to the Treasurer of and for the use of the Municipality. 29-30 V. c. 51, s. 355 (17).

19. If the owner, within forty-eight hours after the delivery of such statements, as provided in the fifth section, disputes the amount of the damages so claimed, the amount shall be decided by the majority of three Fence-viewers of the Municipality, one to be named by the owner of the animal, one by the person distraining or claiming damages, and the third by the Pound-keeper. 29-30 V. c. 51, s. 355 (18).

20. Such Fence-viewers or any two of them shall, within twenty-four hours after notice of their appointment as aforesaid, view the fence and the ground upon which the animal was found doing damage, and determine whether or not the fence was a lawful one according to the statutes or by-laws in that behalf at the time of the trespass ; and if it was a lawful fence, then they shall appraise the damages commit-

ted, and, within twenty-four hours after having made the view, shall deliver to the Pound-keeper a written statement signed by at least two of them of their appraisement, and of their lawful fees and charges. 29-30 V. c. 51, s. 355 (19).

21. If the Fence-viewers decide that the fence was not a lawful one, they shall certify the same in writing under their hands, together with a statement of their lawful fees to the Pound-keeper, who shall, upon payment of all lawful fees and charges, deliver such animal to the owner if claimed before the sale thereof ; but if not claimed, or if such fees and charges are not paid, the Pound-keeper, after due notice, as required by this Act, shall sell the animal in the manner before mentioned at the time and place appointed in the notices. 29-30 V. c. 51, s. 355 (21).

22. In case any Pound-keeper or person who impounds or confines, or causes to be impounded or confined, any animal as aforesaid, refuses or neglects to find, provide and supply the animal with good and sufficient food, water and shelter as aforesaid, he shall, for every day during which he so refuses or neglects, forfeit a sum not less than one dollar nor more than four dollars. 29-30 V. c. 51, s. 355 (22).

23. Any Fence-viewer neglecting his duty as arbitrator as aforesaid, shall incur a penalty of two dollars, to be recovered for the use of the Municipality, by summary proceedings before a Justice of the Peace upon the complaint of the party aggrieved, or the Treasurer of the Municipality. 29-30 V. c. 51, s. 355 (20).

24. Every fine and penalty imposed by this Act may be recovered and enforced, with costs, by summary conviction, before any Justice of the Peace for the County, or of the Municipality in which the offence was committed ; and, in default of payment, the offender may be committed to the Common Gaol, House of Correction, or Lock-up House of such County or Municipality, there to be imprisoned for any time, in the discretion of the convicting and committing Justice, not exceeding fourteen days, unless such fine and penalty, and costs, including the costs of the committal, are sooner paid. 29-30 V. c. 51, s. 355, (23).

25. When not otherwise provided, every pecuniary penalty recovered before any Justice of the Peace under this Act shall be paid and distributed in the following manner : one moiety to the City, Town, Village or Township in which the offence was committed, and the other moiety thereof, with full costs, to the person who informed and prosecuted for the same, or to such other person as to the Justice seems proper. 29-30 V. c. 51, s. 355 (25).

BY-LAW No. 6 OF 1886.

A By-law to restrain and regulate the running at large of Dogs, and to impose a tax on the owners, possessors, or harborers of Dogs, and for killing dogs running at large contrary to this By-law.

The Council of the Corporation of the Township of Derby in the County of Grey, enacts as follows :

1. Every owner, possessor, or harborer of a dog within the Township of Derby, shall be liable to pay the sum of one dollar yearly for each dog owned, possessed or harbored ; and for each bitch owned, possessed

or harbored within the Municipality, the owner, possessor or harborer shall be liable to pay the sum of two dollars yearly.

2. It shall be the duty of the Assessor to enter upon the Assessment Roll (in columns to be kept for that purpose) opposite their respective names, the number of dogs or bitches owned, possessed or harbored by every person assessed within the Township of Derby.

3. It shall be the duty of the Township Collector to collect from every person entered upon the assessment Roll as the owner, possessor or harborer of a dog or dogs, bitch or bitches, the sum of one dollar for each dog, and two dollars for each bitch ; and he shall have authority to collect the said amounts the same as any other Township rate ; and the money, when so collected, shall form part of the general funds of the Township.

4. It shall not be lawful for any dog or bitch to run at large from the premises where owned or harbored at any time within the Township of Derby, unless accompanied by his owner or one of his family, or some responsible person, and at a distance of more than forty rods from such person or premises shall be deemed running at large.

5. The owner or harborer of any dog or bitch, which is in the habit of running at large as aforesaid, upon being notified of such habit, shall, in addition to being liable for all damages done or caused to be done by such dog or bitch, be liable to a penalty for every time that such dog or bitch is found running at large.

6. It shall be unlawful for any person or persons to keep or harbor any dog or bitch that is in the habit of annoying travellers passing on the highways, and the owner or harborer of any such dog or bitch, shall be liable for any damage caused by such annoyance, and shall also be liable to a penalty for every time that the annoyance is repeated, after being notified that such dog or bitch is guilty of such a habit ; and the Justice of the Peace before whom complaint is made under this section, may order the dog or bitch guilty of such habit to be destroyed, and may order the owner or harborer to deliver such dog or bitch to a constable, so to be destroyed.

7. If any dog or bitch running at large, contrary to this by-law, shall attack any person travelling on any street, highway or public place in the Township, or do any damage whatsoever, and complaint thereof shall be made to a Justice of the Peace, such Justice shall enquire into the complaint, and if satisfied such complaint is substantiated, shall fine the owner or harborer, and may, in his discretion, order the dog or bitch to be destroyed, and order the owner or harborer to deliver up to a constable the said dog or bitch, so to be destroyed.

8. All notices given in pursuance of this by-law shall be in writing, signed by the party giving the same.

9. Any dog or bitch known to be rabid shall be immediately destroyed.

10. Any person guilty of any infraction of any of the provisions of this by-law, or of refusing or neglecting to deliver up to a constable on order of a Justice of the Peace made by authority of this by-law, any dog or bitch to be destroyed, shall upon conviction before any Justice or Justices of the Peace, for the County of Grey, forfeit and pay at the discretion of the said Justice or Justices convicting, a penalty not

exceeding the sum of fifty dollars for each offence, exclusive of costs ; and in default of payment thereof forthwith, the Justice or Justices convicting as aforesaid, or any one of them, may issue a warrant under his hand and seal, to levy the said penalty and costs by distress and sale of the offender's goods and chattels and in case of no sufficient distress to satisfy the said penalty and costs, the Justice or Justices convicting as aforesaid, or any one of them, may commit the offender or offenders to the Common Gaol of the County of Grey, with or without hard labor for any period not exceeding twenty-one days, unless such fine and penalty and costs, including the costs of the committal, are sooner paid.

11. All By-laws or parts of By-laws of this Corporation, which are contrary to or inconsistent with the provisions of this By-law, shall be and the same are hereby repealed.

JOHN ROBERTSON, Reeve.
W. BEATON, Clerk.

Passed 6th Feb., 1886.

BY-LAW No. 7 of 1886.

Respecting Statute Labor.

The Corporation of the Township of Derby, in the County of Grey, enacts as follows :

1. Any person (resident or non-resident) liable to statute labor within the Municipality of the Township of Derby, are hereby empowered to compound for such labor, for any term not exceeding five years, at the sum of one dollar for each day's labor.

2. The sum of one dollar for each day's labor shall be paid in commutation of such statute labor in the Township of Derby.

3. Every person assessed upon the Assessment Roll of the Township of Derby, shall, if his property is assessed at more than $400, be liable to 2 day's statute labor ;

At more than $400, but not more than $800, 3 days ;
At more than $800, but not more than $1200, 4 days ;
At more than $1200, but not more than $1600, 5 days ;
At more than $1600, but not more than $2200, 6 days ;
At more than $2200, but not more than $2800, 7 days ;
And for every $800 over $2800, or fractional part thereof
over $600, one additional day.

4. Every male inhabitant of the Township, of the age of twenty-one years and upwards and under sixty, who is not otherwise assessed to any amount, and who is not exempt by law from performing statute labor, shall be liable to two day's labor on the roads and highways of the Township ; and it shall be the duty of Overseers to enter the names of all such within their respective divisions on their lists, and to give them or him, as the case may be, at least six clear days' notice of the time and place where the statute labor is to be performed ; and in case of default or refusal to perform such labor, he or they may be proceeded against for an infraction of this By-law.

5. Any person or persons, assessed or otherwise, who prefer paying the commutation tax in lieu of performing statute labor, must pay the

same to the Overseer in whose division such persons or property are
situated, on or before the first day of June in each year.

6. When the amount of commutation received by the Overseer
exceeds ten dollars, it shall be his duty to expend the amount in
improving the roads by public competition ; when under ten dollars,
it may be let by private contract, or by hiring men by the day when
the regular statute labor is being performed.

7. The following regulations shall be adopted for governing Overseers
of Highways in the discharge of their duties :

(1.) To make declaration of office within twenty days from notice of
appointment.

(2.) To take charge of the roads in their respective divisions
immediately after making such declaration, and continue in charge
until their successors are qualified.

(3.) To keep the roads in their respective divisions in such a state
of repair as the labor at their disposal will admit of.

(4.) In cases of special emergency, to call out such persons liable to
perform statute labor as may be necessary to make roads through
snow drifts, remove obstructions or nuisances of any kind, and to
repair culverts, bridges, or other portions of road within their respective
divisions as may be in such a state as to seriously impede the travel
on the same, and to allow the time so expended as statute labor on
the first labor due after the performance of such labor.

(5.) To give reasonable notice, not less than three days, to those
assessed on their lists, of the time and place where the regular statute
labor is to be performed.

(6.) To require persons liable to perform statute labor in their
respective divisions to bring with them such teams, implements and
tools as they may possess to perform such labor.

(7.) To exercise due care and diligence in causing all road work of a
permanent character to be performed on the centre portion of the
allowance for road, and in a straight course.

(8.) To see that each man and team shall perform their fair share of
the work, and in cases of either being inadequate, to charge them with
the deficiency, either by causing them to make it good in labor, or by
returning it as unperformed labor.

(9.) In cases where gravel is purchased by the yard, to keep an
accurate account of the number of yards used under their supervision,
and to certify the same, and from whose pit obtained, on their lists.

(10.) To give those rated on their lists an opportunity of nominating
a person for the office of Overseer for the following year.

(11.) To make their returns to the Township Clerk on or before the
twelfth day of July in each year, of all the labor that has been
performed in their respective divisions, of all moneys received for road
purposes, and how and where expended, and of all work yet unperformed, and why unperformed.

(12.) And generally to perform all duties imposed on them by any
other By-law or Statute.

8. Eight hours faithful work by an able bodied man shall be
reckoned as one day of statute labor, and one day's work of a team
shall be equivalent to a day's work of a man ; and a day's work of a team

with a competent teamster and a wagon or any other implement required after a team, will be reckoned as three day's of labor ; and no allowance will be made for any tools or implements that are used without a team.

9. Any person or persons guilty of an infraction of any of the provisions of this By-law, shall upon conviction before any Justice or Justices of the Peace, on the oath or affirmation of any credible witness, forfeit and pay at the discretion of the said Justice or Justices convicting, a penalty not exceeding the sum of fifty dollars for each offence, exclusive of costs ; and in default of payment thereof forthwith, it shall and may be lawful for the Justice convicting as aforesaid, to issue a warrant under his hand and seal ; or in case any two Justices are acting together therein, then under the hand and seal of one of them, to levy the said penalty and costs, or costs only, by distress and sale of the goods and chattels of the offender or offenders ; and in case of no sufficient distress to satisfy the said penalty and costs, it shall and may be lawful for the Justice aforesaid to commit the offender or offenders to the common gaol of the County of Grey, with or without hard labor, for any period not exceeding twenty-one days, unless the said penalty and costs, including costs of committal, be sooner paid ; and no person shall be exempt from the performance of statute labor on account of having paid a fine or suffered imprisonment on account of the non-performance of the same.

10. All By-laws or parts of By-laws of this Corporation contrary to the provisions of this By-law, are hereby repealed.

JOHN ROBERTSON, REEVE.
W. BEATON, CLERK.

Passed 6th Feb., 1886.

BY-LAW No. 8 OF 1886.

A By-law for enforcing the provisions of " An Act respecting Snow Fences," and for encouraging the construction of Wire Fences in certain places.

Whereas it is desirable and expedient to enforce the provisions of the Act entitled "An Act respecting Snow Fences," and to encourage the construction of Wire Fences along the lines of highway in places subject to accumulations of snow drifts.

Therefore the Corporation of the Township of Derby, in the County of Grey, enacts as follows :

1. The Provincial Statute Forty-four Victoria, Chapter Twenty-six, entitled " An Act respecting Snow Fences," shall be in force in this Township, except so far as varied or regulated by this By-law.

2. In order to encourage the construction of Wire Fences in pursuance of the above-mentioned Act, in places where it is clearly proved to the Council that it will be an improvement to the road, the sum of twenty cents per rod may be granted out of the Township funds to assist any person or persons in erecting Wire Fences in places certified and recommended by at least three ratepayers residing in the neighborhood of the piece of road for which application for said grant is made ; such certificate to accompany the application, and to be in writing, and in the form attached hereto or a form to the like effect.

3. Fences erected in pursuance of the preceding section must be constructed with not less than three strands of wire—the lowest not to be more than eighteen inches from the ground ; must be finished in a substantial and workmanlike manner, and to the satisfaction of the person or committee appointed by the Council to inspect the same ; and in no case shall an order be issued for the payment of the grant until a written certificate of the satisfactory completion and measurement of the fence is handed in.

4. It shall be the duty of Overseers of Highways and the privilege of any ratepayer, to report to the Council or Road and Bridge Committee the places on the roads in their respective divisions that are subject to snow drifts ; and the Council may take such action on said reports as they may deem necessary for the benefit of the roads reported on.

5. The enacting clauses of the Act above referred to ; also the form of application mentioned in section two of this By-law, shall be attached hereto and shall form part of the same.

6. By-law No. 7 of 1885, respecting Snow Fences, is hereby repealed.

JOHN ROBERTSON, Reeve.
W. BEATON, Clerk.

Passed 6th February, 1886.

(44 Vic., Chap. 26.)

AN ACT RESPECTING SNOW FENCES.

1. The Council of every Township, City, Town, or Incorporated Village shall have power to require any owners or occupiers of lands bordering upon any public highway within the Township, to take down, alter or remove any fence or fences, found to cause an accumulation of snow or drifts so as to impede or obstruct the travel on such public highway, or any part thereof, and shall make such compensation to such owners or occupants for the taking down, alteration or removal of such fence or fences, and for the construction of some other description of fence approved of by the Council, in lieu of the one so required to be taken down, altered or removed, as may be mutually agreed upon. And if the Council and the owners or occupants cannot agree in respect to the compensation to be paid by the Council, then the same shall be settled by arbitration in the manner provided by the Municipal Act, and the award so made shall be binding upon all the parties.

2. In case any such owner or occupant shall refuse or neglect to take down, alter or remove such fence or fences as required by the Council, the Council may, after the expiration of two months from the time the compensation to be paid by the Council has been agreed upon or settled by arbitration, proceed to take down, alter or remove the old fence and construct the other description of fence which has been approved of by the Council ; and the amount of all costs and charges thereby incurred by the Council, over and above the amount of compensation agreed upon or settled by arbitration, may immediately be recovered from such owner or occupier by action in any Division Court

having jurisdiction in the locality, and the amount of the judgment in favor of the municipality obtained in such Court shall, if not sooner paid, be by the Clerk of the municipality placed upon the next Collector's roll as taxes against the lands upon or along the boundaries of which the said fence is situate, and after being placed upon the Collector's roll shall be collected and treated in all respects as other taxes imposed by the By-laws of the municipality. When a tenant or occupant other than the owner shall be required to pay the aforesaid sum or any part thereof, such tenant or occupant may deduct the same and any costs paid by him from the rent payable by him, or may otherwise recover the same, unless such tenant or occupant shall have agreed with the landlord to pay the same.

FORM REFERRED TO IN SECTION 2 OF BY-LAW No. 8 OF 1886.

To the Reeve and Council of the Township of Derby :—

GENTLEMEN :—In pursuance of By-law No. 8 of 1886, we, the undersigned ratepayers, hereby certify that we are well acquainted with the piece of road commencing at   and ending at   opposite the property of   , and that owing to its exposed situation, has in times of snow storms been subject to heavy drifts ; we therefore recommend that the assistance provided for under said By-law be granted to   as we consider that the erection of a Wire Fence along the   side of said road would materially lessen the difficulty heretofore experienced in travelling over said road during heavy snow storms.

[Signed]   ————————————

————————————

————————————

Derby,   18

BY-LAW No. 9 OF 1886.

A By-law for preventing the placing of obstructions on the Highways of the Township of Derby, and for other purposes therein mentioned.

Be it enacted by the Corporation of the Township of Derby, in the County of Grey, as follows :

1. It shall be unlawful for any person or persons to place any obstructions, such as cordwood, saw logs, or any other material, and allow the same to remain on the public highways of the Township of Derby.

2. It shall be unlawful for any person or persons to dig holes in any of the Township roads, or to remove any earth, sand, or gravel from the same, without the permission of the Overseer of Highways, in whose Division the same is situated, expressed in writing ; and such permission shall only be given on the express condition that the person or persons removing the earth, sand, or gravel as aforesaid, shall be held responsible for any inconvenience or damage that may be sustained by the travelling public while he or they are in the act of removing

the same ; and also on the condition that the holes or pitfalls made by the removal of the same shall be properly filled in by the person removing the same, so as not to render the road in the vicinity of where the holes are made dangerous for either man or beast.

3. It shall be unlawful for any person or persons to drag any logs or other substance along any of the highways or across any of the bridges within the Township of Derby, whereby any injury may be done to such roads or bridges.

4. It shall be unlawful for the owner or owners of any animal or animals that may die by accident or otherwise, on the public highways of the Township of Derby, or contiguous thereto, to allow or permit the carcase or carcases of such animals to remain on the highway or within view or close proximity to the same ; but shall immediately upon ascertaining that the animal or animals as aforesaid are dead, cause the carcase or carcases to be removed out of sight from the highway and buried or destroyed by fire or otherwise, so as to effectually prevent any offensive smell to be felt by the travelling public or the people residing in the vicinity of where they are interred or destroyed.

5. Any damage sustained by any person or persons travelling or driving on the highways of the Township of Derby, in consequence of any of the causes mentioned in sections one, two, three and four of this By-law, may be recovered from the person or persons through whose default or neglect the cause of damage was occasioned.

6. It shall be the duty of Overseers of Highways, with or without complaint being made to them by any ratepayer or other person, to cause the provisions of this By-law to be observed in their respective Divisions, and to prosecute any person or persons guilty of a breach of or refusing to comply with its provisions.

7. Any person or persons guilty of an infraction of any of the provisions of this By-law, shall upon conviction before any Justice or Justices of the Peace on the oath or affirmation of any credible witness, forfeit and pay, at the discretion of the said Justice or Justices convicting, a penalty not exceeding the sum of fifty dollars for each offence, exclusive of costs ; and in default of payment thereof forthwith, it shall and may be lawful for the Justice convicting as aforesaid, to issue a warrant under his hand and seal ; or in case any two Justices are acting together therein, then under the hand and seal of one of them ; to levy the said penalty and costs, or costs only, by distress and sale of the goods and chattels of the offender or offenders ; and in case of no sufficient distress to satisfy the said penalty and costs, it shall and may be lawful for the Justice aforesaid, to commit the offender or offenders to the Common Gaol of the County of Grey, with or without hard labor, for any period not exceeding twenty-one days, unless the said penalty and costs, including costs of committal, be sooner paid.

JOHN ROBERTSON, Reeve.
W. BEATON, Clerk.

Passed 6th Feb., 1886.

BY-LAW No. 10 OF 1886.

A By-law for the removal of Fences and other obstructions on Highways.

The Corporation of the Township of Derby enacts as follows :

1. Any person in possession of a road allowance in the cases stated in section 552 of the "Consolidated Municipal Act of 1883," when the same is opened by By-law under section 553, shall within such time as the Council may order, remove any fence or other obstruction enclosing or obstructing the same.

2. It shall be unlawful for any person to enclose by a fence or other obstruction any other Highway or any part thereof in the Township.

3. No person shall travel on horseback or in vehicles on so much of any Highway as the Council have or may hereafter set apart for the purposes of a footpath.

4. Any person guilty of an infraction of this By-law shall on conviction thereof be liable to a fine or penalty not exceeding fifty dollars, exclusive of costs ; and in default of payment thereof and costs forthwith, the said penalty and costs to be collected by distress and sale of the goods and chattels of the offender ; and in case no distress be found out of which such fine can be levied, the offender may be imprisoned with or without hard labor in the Common Gaol of the County of Grey for any period not exceeding twenty-one days, unless the said penalty and costs, including the costs of committal, be sooner paid.

5. Any By-law or parts of By-laws heretofore enacted whose provisions are contrary to or inconsistent with the provisions of this By-law, are hereby repealed.

JOHN ROBERTSON, Reeve.
W. BEATON, Clerk.

Passed 6th February, 1886.

Sections 552 and 553 of the Consolidated Municipal Act of 1883.

POSSESSION OF UNOPENED ROAD ALLOWANCES.

552. In case a person is in possession of any part of a government allowance for road laid out adjoining his lot and enclosed by a lawful fence, and which has not been opened for public use by reason of another road being used in lieu thereof ; or is in possession of any government allowance for road parallel or near to which a road has been established by law in lieu thereof, such person shall be deemed legally possessed thereof, as against any private person, until a by-law has been passed for opening such allowance for road by the Council having jurisdiction over the same. R. S. O. c. 174, s. 511. (36 V. c. 48, s. 427.)

NOTICE OF BY-LAWS FOR OPENING SUCH ALLOWANCES.

553. No such by-law shall be passed until notice in writing has been given to the person in possession, at least eight days before the meeting of the Council, that an application will be made for opening such allowance. R. S. O. c. 174, s. 512. (36 V. c. 48, s. 428.)

BY-LAW No. 11 of 1886.

To prevent the Obstruction of Streams, Creeks, and Water-courses by Trees, Brushwood, Timber, or other materials, and for clearing away and removing such obstructions at the expense of the Offenders or otherwise ; and for making provisions for levying the expense if not otherwise paid in the same manner as taxes are paid.

Be it enacted by the Corporation of the Township of Derby in the County of Grey, as follows :

1. It shall be unlawful for any person or persons to cause trees, brushwood, timber, or any other material to be felled or placed in any of the streams, creeks, or water courses within the Municipality of the Township of Derby.

2. In cases where trees, brushwood, timber or any other materials are placed or found in any of the streams, creeks, or water-courses within the Township of Derby to such an extent as to cause injury or damage to any lands or other property in consequence of the backing of water, the owner or owners (when known) of the property where such obstructions are placed or found, shall, on receiving notice in writing (*Form* 1) before the first day of August in each year from any person or persons interested in lands injuriously affected in consequence of such obstructions, cause so much of them as have actually been placed there by him or them to be removed before the first day of October next ensuing : provided always that no person will be liable for obstructions through natural causes over which he had no control.

3. In cases where owners of property where obstructions are placed or found in any of the streams, creeks, and water-courses as aforesaid neglect or refuse to remove the same when notified as aforesaid, or in case where the owner or owners are unknown, the owners or other parties interested in lands injuriously affected by such obstructions may apply to three Fence-viewers of the Municipality (*Form* 2) for the purpose of arbitrating upon the extent of damage, if any, caused by such obstructions, and estimating the probable cost of removing the same.

4. The Fence-viewers upon receiving such application shall meet at the time and place mentioned therein, and shall enquire into and report on the following particulars :

(1.) The extent of damage, if any, caused to the lands of the applicant or applicants by reason of such obstructions.

(2.) The probable cost of removing them.

(3.) The proportion of costs that should be borne by the party or parties on whose property the obstructions are placed or found.

(4.) The proportion of costs, if any, that should be borne by the party or parties whose properties are likely to be benefitted by the removal of such obstructions.

(5.) The amount of their own fees, and on what properties or persons the same are to be levied.

(6.) Their opinion as to the propriety or advisability of enforcing the removal of such obstructions.

5. The Fence-viewers shall make their award (*Form* 3) embracing the particulars contained in the foregoing section, and shall cause it to be delivered to the Township Clerk forthwith.

6. In cases where the award of the Fence-viewers indicates the propriety of enforcing the removal of obstructions as aforesaid, and the Council consider it of sufficient importance to warrant them in doing so, they shall instruct the Ditches and Water-courses Engineer to proceed to remove them either by letting the job by public competition or by employing men by the day, as to him may seem most judicious, according to the nature of the work.

7. The Engineer shall report to the Council the actual costs of removing the obstructions, and the Clerk shall levy the same on the lands, and in the proportion pointed out by the Fence-viewers' Award, and shall place them on the Collectors' Roll made next thereafter, the same as other taxes ; and the Council in the meantime shall pay the costs of arbitration by the Fence-viewers, and those of removing the obstructions out of the general funds of the Township.

8. Any person or persons guilty of an infraction of any of the provisions of this By-law, shall upon conviction before any Justice or Justices of the Peace, on the oath or affirmation of any credible witness, forfeit and pay at the discretion of the said Justice or Justices convicting, a penalty not exceeding the sum of fifty dollars for each offence, exclusive of costs ; and in default of payment thereof forthwith, it shall and may be lawful for the Justice convicting as aforesaid to issue a warrant under his hand and seal : or in case any two Justices are acting together therein, then under the hand and seal of one of them, to levy the said penalty and costs, or costs only, by distress and sale of the goods and chattels of the offender or offenders ; and in case of no sufficient distress to satisfy the said penalty and costs, it shall and may be lawful for the Justice aforesaid to commit the offender or offenders to the Common Gaol of the County of Grey, with or without hard labor, for any period not exceeding twenty-one days, unless the said penalty and costs, including costs of committal, be sooner paid.

9. The forms attached to this By-law, or forms to the like effect, will be deemed sufficient for the purposes thereof, and shall be taken and held as being part of the same.

10. All By-laws or parts of By-laws of this Corporation, which are contrary to or inconsistent with the provisions of this By-law, shall be and the same are hereby repealed.

JOHN ROBERTSON, Reeve.
W. BEATON, Clerk.

Passed 6th Feb., 1886.

Notices Referred to in the Foregoing By-law.

(FORM 1.)

Take notice that in pursuance of By-law No. 11 of 1886 of the Township of Derby, I require you to remove the obstructions placed by you, and now lying in the (*stream, creek, or water-course, as the case may be*) on Lot   in the   concession of this Township, so as to allow the water to have its free course in its natural channel; and in default of your not doing so and having the same completed on or before the first day of October next, take notice that I will apply to the Fence-viewers to deal with the matter according to the provisions of the said By-law

Dated Derby, this   day of   18

To—————————   A. B., Complainant.

(FORM 2)

Application to Fence-viewers.

In conformity with the provisions of By-law No. 11 of 1886 of the Township of Derby, I hereby make application and require you to attend at lot   in the   concession, on   the   day of   18   at   o'clock, to view and arbitrate on the extent of damage or otherwise caused to the following property, viz :   by reason of certain obstructions placed and found lying in the (*stream, etc., etc.*) on said lot, and request you to deal with it and make your award according to the true intent and meaning of said By-law,

Dated at   this   day of   18

To ————————— , Fence-viewer.   C. D., Complainant.

(FORM 3.)

Award of Fence-viewers.

We, the undersigned Fence-viewers of the Township of Derby, having received application from   in pursuance of By-law No. 11 of 1886 of the Township of Derby, to view and arbitrate upon the injurious effects of certain obstructions alleged to be placed and found lying in (*the stream, creek, or water-course as the case may be*) on lot   in the   concession of the Township of Derby ; and having examined the premises, do hereby, according to the provisions of said By-law, award as follows (*here state the particulars asked in section 4.*)

Given under our hands at the Township of Derby, this   day of   18

—————————— ; ⎫
—————————— ; ⎬ Fence-viewers.
—————————— ; ⎭

BY-LAW No. 12 of 1886,

To regulate the times during which stumps, wood, logs, trees, brush, straw, shavings or refuse may be set on fire or burned in the open air ; and for prescribing precautions to be observed during such times, and for preventing fires being kindled at other times.

—

The Corporation of the Township of Derby, in the County of Grey, enacts as follows :

1. Stumps, wood, logs and brush may be set on fire in the open air in any month during the year, excepting the month of August.

2. Trees, straw, shavings or refuse may be set on fire and burned in the open air after sundown on a calm evening in any month during the year, excepting the month of August.

3. The following precautions must be observed by any person or persons setting on fire any of the materials mentioned in the first and second sections of this By-law.

(1.) If the material to be burned is within twenty rods of any neighbor's fences or buildings, or a division line fence between neighbors, the person or persons setting out the fire must give at least one day's notice to all the persons owning, occupying or interested in fences or buildings within the said limit, of his or their intention of setting out the fire ; such notices must be in writing, and state the time and place when and where the fire is intended to be set out.

(2.) The person or persons setting out the fire must use due diligence in preventing it from spreading ; and in case of it spreading must assist in checking it on any premises it may reach.

4. It shall be unlawful for any person or persons to set out fire to burn in the open air, any stumps, wood, logs, trees, brush, straw, shavings or refuse, or any other inflamable material during the month of August.

5. Any person or persons setting out fire in the fields or bush or on the roads or commons of the Township of Derby, contrary to the provisions of this By-law, shall in addition to being held responsible for any damage occasioned thereby, be liable upon conviction before any Justice or Justices of the Peace on the oath or affirmation of any credible witness, to forfeit and pay at the discretion of the said Justice or Justices convicting, a penalty not exceeding the sum of fifty dollars for each offence, exclusive of costs ; and in default of payment thereof forthwith, it shall and may be lawful for the Justice convicting as aforesaid to issue a warrant under his hand and seal ; or in case any two Justices are acting together therein, then under the hand and seal of one of them, to levy the said penalty and costs, or costs only, by distress and sale of the goods and chattels of the offender or offenders ; and in case of no sufficient distress to satisfy the said penalty and costs, it shall and may be lawful for the Justice aforesaid to commit the offender or offenders to the Common Gaol of the County of Grey, with or without hard labor, for any period not exceeding twenty-one days, unless the said penalty and costs, including costs of committal, be sooner paid.

JOHN ROBERTSON, Reeve.
W. BEATON, Clerk.

Passed 6th February, 1886.

BY-LAW No. 13 OF 1886,

For authorizing the payment of a bonus or premium for the encourage-
ment of the planting and growing of trees, under the authority of
" The Ontario Tree Planting Act, 1883," and amendments thereto;
and for authorizing the appointment of an Inspector of trees so
planted, and making certain regulations in connection therewith.

Be it enacted by the Municipal Council of the Corporation of the
Township of Derby, in the County of Grey, as follows :

1. A bonus of twenty cents shall be paid out of the funds of this
Corporation for each tree, certified by the inspector of Trees, to be
planted and growing, in pursuance of " The Ontario Tree Planting Act,
1883," and amendments thereto, on any of the highways or on any
boundary line of farms within the Township of Derby.

2. An Inspector of Trees shall be appointed in pursuance of the said
Act, who shall be deemed an officer of this Corporation ; and the said
Inspector shall continue in office until he resigns or is removed by the
Council.

3. It shall be the Inspector's duty before granting a certificate to
any person or persons who have planted trees in pursuance of said Act,
to ascertain,

(1.) That no species of trees that he and the Council may deem
unsuitable are planted ;

(2.) That the trees planted on the highways are so planted in order
hereinafter specified as to the distance from the boundary line, and
the distance apart, and that they are so planted in a straight line ;

(3.) That they are securely protected and in a healthy and thrifty
condition, in good form, and not less than one and a quarter inches in
diameter, and not less than seven nor more than ten feet in height.

4. The regulations authorized by the Consolidated Municipal Act of
1883, section 482, sub-section 22, shall be in force under this By-law ;
also the penalties provided for under section 9 of " The Ontario Tree
Planting Act, 1883," both of which sections are hereto annexed, and
are to be taken as forming part of this By-law.

5. The following regulations shall be in force respecting the planting
of trees on the public highways or on boundary lines, within the
Township of Derby :

(1.) The distance that trees may be planted from the boundary line
on the highways shall be six feet, and the distance from one tree and
the tree nearest thereto shall be thirty feet, and in all cases the trees
are to be planted in a straight line.

(2.) No trees shall be planted, under the authority of this By-law,
on the public highways, of any species that the Council or their
Inspector may deem unsuited for the purpose.

(3.) Persons planting trees on the public highways contrary to the
regulations of this By-law, and also to the true intent and meaning of
" The Ontario Tree Planting Act, 1883," will not be entitled to a
bonus or premium ; and the Inspector shall not include such in his
report of those entitled to the same ; and it shall be lawful for the
Council to remove or forbid the removal of such trees by special
resolution as to them may seem expedient.

6. Sections four, five, six and seven, with the amendments thereto, of "The Ontario Tree Planting Act, 1883," attached hereto, shall be in force under this By-law, and shall be printed together with copies of the same.

7. All By-laws or parts of By-laws, inconsistent with the provisions of this By-law, are hereby repealed.

JOHN ROBERTSON, Reeve.
W. BEATON, Clerk.

Passed 6th Feb., 1886.

"THE ONTARIO TREE PLANTING ACT—1883."

(Sections 4, 5, 6 and 7.)

4. Any person owning land adjacent to any highway, or to any public street, lane, alley, place or square in this Province, may plant trees on the portion thereof contiguous to his land ; but no tree shall be so planted that the same is or may become a nuisance in the highway or other public thoroughfare, or obstruct the fair and reasonable use of the same.

(2.) Any owner of a farm or lot of land may, with the consent of the owner or owners of adjoining lands, plant trees on the boundary lines of his farm or lot.

(3.) Every such tree so planted on any such highway, street, lane, alley, place or square, shall be deemed to be the property of the owner of the lands adjacent to such highway, street, lane, alley, place or square, and nearest to such tree ; and every such tree so planted on a boundary line aforesaid, shall be deemed to be the common property of the owners of the adjoining farms or lots.

(4.) Every growing tree, shrub or sapling, whatsoever planted or left standing on either side of any highway for the purposes of shade or ornament shall, upon, from, and after the passing of this Act, be deemed to be the property of the owner of the land adjacent to such highway and nearest to such tree, shrub or sapling. (Substituted pursuant to 47 Vic. chap. 36.)

2. Any person who ties or fastens any animal to, or injures or destroys any tree growing for the purposes of shade or ornament upon any boundary line between farms or lots, or who suffers or permits any animal in his charge to injure or destroy, or who cuts down or removes any such tree without the consent of the owner or owners of such tree, shall be subject to the like penalties, and liable to be proceeded against, and dealt with as provided in section 9 of the said Act. 47 Vic., chap. 36, sec. 2.

5. The Council of any Municipality may pass a By-law for paying out of Municipal funds a bonus or premium not exceeding twenty-five cents for each and every ash, basswood, beech, birch, butternut, cedar, cherry, chestnut, elm, hickory, maple, oak, pine, sassafras, spruce, walnut, or whitewood tree, which shall, under the provisions of this Act, be planted within such Municipality on any highway, or on any boundary line of farms as aforesaid, or within six feet of such boundary.

(2.) Such By-law shall further provide for the appointment of an inspector of trees so planted ; for their due protection against injury and against removal by any person or persons, including the owner, excepting as authority may be given therefor by special resolution of the Council ; for the conditions on which bonuses may be paid ; and generally for such regulations as are authorized by chapter one hundred and seventy-four of the Revised Statutes of Ontario, section 454 (16.)

(3.) Printed copies of the said By-law, together with sections four, five, six and seven of this Act, shall be posted throughout the Municipality, and all claims made to the Council under the provisions of the By-law shall be referred to the inspector to obtain proof of the same and report thereon.

6. The inspector shall make to the Council one report for each year, if required so to do, giving the names of all persons entitled to any bonus or premium under the By-law, the number of trees of each species planted, and the amount of bonus or premium to which each person is entitled, and certifying that the distance between any one tree and the tree nearest thereto is not less than thirty feet, that the trees have been planted for a period of three years, and that they are alive, healthy and of good form ; and upon the adoption of such report the bonuses or premiums shall be paid.

7. The Treasurer of the Province, upon receiving a copy of the inspector's report, certified by the Reeve and Clerk, shall recoup to the treasurer of the Municipality one-half of the sum paid by the Municipality under the authority of this Act, the said copy to be forwarded on or before the first day of November in each year.

MUNICIPAL ACT OF 1883, SECTION 482, SUB-SECTION 22.

ORNAMENTAL TREES.

For causing any tree, shrub, or sapling, growing or planted on any public place, square, highway, street, lane, alley, or other communication under its control, to be removed, if and when such removal is deemed necessary for any purpose of public improvement ; but no such tree, shrub or sapling shall be so removed until after one month's notice thereof is given to the owner of the adjoining property, and he is recompensed for his trouble in planting and protecting the same ; nor shall such owner, or any pathmaster or other public officer, or any other person, remove or cut down or injure such tree, shrub or sapling on pretence of improving the public place, square, highway, street, road, lane, alley or other communication or otherwise, without the express permission of the Municipal Council having the control of the public place, square, highway, street, road, lane, alley or other communication ; and any Council may expend money in planting and preserving shade and ornamental trees upon any public place, square, highway, street, road, lane, alley, or other communication within the Municipality, and may grant sums of money to any person or association of persons to be expended for the same purposes.

"THE ONTARIO TREE PLANTING ACT—1883."

PENALTIES.

9. Any person who ties or fastens any animal to or injures or destroys a tree planted and growing upon any road or highway, or upon any public street, lane, alley, place or square in this Province (or upon any boundary line of farms, if any such bonus or premium as aforesaid has been paid therefor), or suffers or permits any animal in his charge to injure or destroy, or who cuts down or removes any such tree without having first obtained permission so to do by special resolution of the Council of the municipality, shall, upon conviction thereof, before a Justice of the Peace, forfeit and pay such sum of money, not exceeding twenty-five dollars, besides costs, as such Justice may award ; and in default of payment the same may be levied of the goods and chattels of the person offending ; or such person may be imprisoned in the Common Gaol of the County within which the municipality is situate for a period not exceeding thirty days.

(2.) One-half of such fine shall go to the person laying the information, and the other half to the municipality within which such tree was growing.

BY-LAW No. 14 OF 1886.

To make Regulations with Reference to the Town Hall.

Be it enacted by the Corporation of the Township of Derby, in the County of Grey, as follows :

1. The occupancy of the Town Hall for any lawful and moral purpose, shall be and is hereby made available to the general public on an application to the Township Treasurer of one or more responsible persons, who shall be held responsible for the character of the meeting or meetings, and the safety of the Hall during the hours or time of meeting.

2. The following rents shall be charged :

(1.) For Religious Services held once each Sabbath, at the rate of ten dollars per annum shall be charged.

(2.) For a lecture on a moral or scientific subject, when an admission fee is charged, one dollar per meeting ; when no admission fee is charged and no collection taken up, it shall be free.

(3.) Travelling shows, concerts, or exhibitions of any kind that are followed as a calling and for gain, two dollars per meeting.

(4.) For night schools of any kind during the winter months, when fuel and light are required, twenty cents per night, and at other seasons when fuel is not required, ten cents per night.

3. The wood for fire, as well as such means of light as are in the Hall to be included in the above charges.

4. Nothing of an immoral tendency shall have permission to occupy the Hall ; and dancing at any social gathering therein is hereby prohibited.

5. The Hall shall be opened by the Caretaker when required for Agricultural, Political and Judicial purposes free of charge.

6. The Treasurer shall be the officer to whom application is to be made for occupying the Hall, and he may require that the rents be paid in advance, and his receipt or permit shown to the Caretaker shall be his authority for opening the Hall.

7. It shall be the Caretaker's duty to look after the safety of the Hall at all times, and to have a personal oversight of it at all meetings held therein ; to attend to sweeping, heating and lighting when required : and in case of a secret society, private meetings or night schools, may demand a responsible person in either case to assume the duties of caretaker during such meetings, and must be allowed free admission to all public meetings or concerts.

9. All By-laws with reference to the Town Hall, inconsistent with the provisions of this By-law, are hereby repealed.

JOHN ROBERTSON, REEVE.
W. BEATON, CLERK.

Passed 6th Feb., 1886.

BY-LAW No. 98,

To provide for inflicting reasonable Fines and Penalties.

Be it enacted by the Corporation of the Township of Derby, in the County of Grey, and it is hereby enacted by the authority of the same as follows :

1. Any person elected or appointed to any office in the said Township of Derby, and who neglects or refuses to perform the duties thereof after he has received notice of his election or appointment, or who has accepted such office and taken the oaths and made the necessary declaration, and afterwards neglects the duties thereof ; or any person who commits a breach of any of the By-laws of the said Township : shall be liable to a penalty or fine of not less than one dollar nor more than fifty dollars, exclusive of costs : provided that any person who has filled an office shall not be required to serve in the same more than once in three years against his will ; but this provision shall not apply to a person who has taken the declaration of office and afterwards neglects the duties thereof.

2. Any penalty or fine and costs that may be imposed for any breach of a By-law, or under this By-law, may be collected by distress and sale of the goods and chattels of the offender ; and in the event of there being no distress out of which such fine and costs can be levied, then such offender may be imprisoned, with or without hard labour, in any lock-up house in the Township, or in the County Gaol, for any period not exceeding twenty-one days.

3. This By-law shall be applicable to offences against By-laws heretofore made or hereinafter to be made.

(L.S.)   JOHN McINNIS, REEVE.
WM. BEATON, CLERK.

Council Room, Derby, 9th July, 1864.

CHAPTER 27—ONTARIO STATUTES, 1883.

AN ACT RESPECTING DITCHES AND WATERCOURSES

[*Assented to 1st February*, 1883.]

Her Majesty, by and with the advice and consent of the Legislative Assembly of the Province of Ontario, enacts as follows :

1. This Act may be cited as "The Ditches and Watercourses Act, 1883."

2. This Act shall not affect the Acts relating to Municipal or Government Drainage.

3. In case of owners of lands, whether immediately adjoining or not, which would be benefitted by making a ditch or drain, or by deepening or widening a ditch or drain already made in a natural watercourse, or by making, deepening or widening a ditch or drain for the purpose of taking off surplus water, or in order to enable the owners or occupiers thereof the better to cultivate or use the same, such several owners shall open and make, deepen or widen a just and fair proportion of such ditch or drain according to their several interests in the construction of the same ; and such ditches or drains shall be kept and maintained so opened, deepened or widened by the said owners respectively and their successors in such ownership in such proportions as they have been so opened, deepened or widened, unless in consequence of altered circumstances the engineer hereinafter named otherwise direct, which he is hereby empowered to do upon application of any party interested, in the same form and manner as is hereinafter prescribed in respect of the original opening, deepening or widening ; and in case the engineer finds no good reason for such application all costs caused thereby shall be borne by the applicant and shall be collected as in this Act provided.

4. Every Municipal Council shall, upon the passing of this Act, name and appoint by By-law an engineer to carry out the provisions of this Act, and such engineer shall be and continue an officer of such corporation until his appointment is repealed by By-law and another engineer appointed in his stead who shall have authority as well to take as to continue any proceeding already commenced under this Act.

5. In case of dispute between owners respecting such proportions any owner shall, before filing with the Clerk of the Municipality the requisition provided for in section six of this Act (Form C or to the like effect), serve upon the other owners or occupants of the lands to be affected a notice in writing signed by him (Form B or to the like effect) naming a day, hour and place convenient to said ditch or drain at which the parties are to meet and, if possible, agree upon the respective portions of such ditch or drain to be made, deepened or widened by each of them, such notice to be served not less than six clear days before time of meeting : and in case at such meeting an agreement shall be come to between the parties, such agreement shall be reduced to writing (Form A or to the like effect), and shall be signed by all the parties ; and shall, within four clear days from the signing thereof, be filed with the Clerk of the Municipality in which

the land requiring such ditch or drain is situate, and such agreement may be enforced in like manner as an award of the engineer as hereinafter provided.

6. In case the parties at such meeting shall not agree, any owner may file with the Clerk of the Municipality in which the lands requiring such ditch or drain is situated a requisition (Form C or to the like effect) shortly describing the ditch or drain to be made, deepened or widened, and naming the lands which will be affected thereby and the owners respectively, and requesting that the engineer appointed by the Municipality for the purpose shall attend at the time and place named in the requisition, which shall not be less than six clear days from the time of filing the same, and shall also at least four clear days before the time appointed therein serve upon all the persons named in such requisition a notice (Form D or to the like effect) requiring their attendance at the said time and place.

7. An occupant not the owner of land, notified in the manner provided by this Act shall immediately notify the owner thereof, and shall, if he neglects to do so, be liable for all damages suffered by such owner by reason of such neglect.

8. The Clerk shall, after receiving such requisition, forthwith notify the said engineer by registered letter enclosing a copy of the said requisition to him, and the engineer shall attend at the time and place named therein ; shall examine the premises, and if he deem proper, or, if requested by any of the parties, shall hear evidence, and is hereby authorized to examine the parties and their witnesses on oath, and may administer an oath or affirmation as in courts of law, and if he shall find the making, deepening, or widening of such ditch or drain necessary, he shall, within thirty days from the receipt of the requisition by him, make his award in writing (Form E or to the like effect) specifying clearly the locality, description and course of said ditch or drain, point of commencement and termination of same, the portion of said ditch or drain to be done by the respective parties and the time within which said work is to be done, the amount of his fees and other charges, and by whom to be paid, and he shall have power to adjourn the said examination, and may require the notification and attendance of other parties whom he deems interested in said ditch or drain, such "other parties" to have at least four clear days notice of time and place of attendance.

9. If it appears to the engineer that the owner or occupier of any tract of land is not sufficiently interested in the opening up of the ditch or drain to make him liable to perform any part thereof, and at the same time that it is necessary for the other parties that such ditch or drain should be continued across such tract, he may award the same to be done at the expense of such other parties, and after such award the said "other parties" may open the ditch or drain across the tract at their own expense without being trespassers ; but causing no unnecessary damage and replacing any fences opened or removed by them.

10. The said engineer shall, when such award is made, file the same and any plan or profile of said work with the Clerk of the Municipality named in section six of this Act, and the award, plan and profile shall be official documents and may be given in evidence in any legal proceedings by certified copies as are other official documents, and the

Clerk of the Municipality shall forthwith, upon the filing of said award, notify each of the persons affected thereby by registered letter or personal service of the filing of the same.

11. Any person dissatisfied with the award and affected thereby may, within ten clear days from the filing thereof, appeal therefrom to the Judge of the County Court of the County in which the lands, in respect to which the proceedings are initiated, are situate, and the proceedings on such appeal shall be as follows :

(1.) The appellant shall serve upon the Clerk of the Municipality with whom the award is filed a notice in writing of his intention to appeal therefrom, shortly setting forth the grounds of appeal.

(2.) The Clerk of said Municipality shall, after the expiration of the time for appeal, forward by registered letter or deliver a copy of such notice, or notices of appeal if there be more than one appeal, to the Clerk of the Division Court of the Division in which the land of the owner filing the requisition as provided in section six of this Act is situate, and such Division Court Clerk shall immediately notify the judge of said appeal, whereupon the judge shall appoint a time for the hearing thereof, and if he think fit, order such sum of money to be paid by the appellant or appellants to the said clerk as will be a sufficient indemnity against costs of the appeal.

(3.) The judge shall order the time and place for hearing of appeals, and communicate the same to the Clerk of the Division Court, who shall notify the engineer and all parties interested in the manner herein provided for the service of other notices under this Act.

(4.) The judge shall hear and determine the appeal or appeals, and set aside, alter or affirm the award, correcting any error therein, and he may examine parties and witnesses on oath and, if he so pleases, inspect the premises, requiring the attendance with him of the Engineer, and may order payment of costs by the parties or any of them, and fix the amount of such costs.

(5.) The award as so altered or confirmed shall be certified by the Clerk of the Division Court to the Clerk of the Municipality, together with the costs, if any, allowed and by whom to be paid, and such award shall be enforced as the award of the engineer, and the time for the completion of the work thereunder shall be computed from the date of such judgment in appeal.

12. The Municipality shall at the expiration of the time for appeal or after appeal, as the case may be, pay to the engineer his fees, and also pay to the person declared to be entitled to the same, any fees or costs awarded or adjudged to him, and shall, unless the same be forthwith repaid by the person awarded or adjudged to pay the same, place the amount upon the collector's roll as a charge against the lands of the person awarded or adjudged to pay the same, and the same shall thereupon become a charge upon such lands, and shall be collected as ordinary Municipal taxes.

13. The engineer shall, at the expiration of the time limited by the award for the completion of the work, inspect the said ditch or drain, if required in writing so to do by any of the parties interested, and if he finds the said work or any portion thereof, not completed in accordance with the award, he may let the same in sections as apportioned in the award to the lowest bidder therefor, taking such security for the performance thereof within the time to be limited, as he may deem

necessary; but no such letting shall take place till after four clear days'
notice in writing of such intended letting has been posted in at least
three conspicuous places in the neighbourhood of the work, and notice
thereof is sent by registered letter to such parties interested in said
award as are non-resident in said Municipality but if the engineer is
satisfied of the bona fides of the person doing the work, and there is
good reason for the non-completion thereof, he may, in his discretion,
extend such time.

14. The engineer shall upon receipt of notice in writing of the final
completion of the work mentioned in the preceding section inspect the
same within one week thereafter, and if approved of, and accepted by
him, certify in writing the fact to the Clerk of the Municipality, giving
a separate certificate for each portion or section of work let and completed (Form F or to the like effect), and stating the name in each certificate of the person who did the work, as well as the amount he is entitled to receive therefor, and also such extra fees as the engineer is
entitled to, by reason of such letting and subsequent inspection, and
by whom the same are to be paid.

15. The Council shall at their meeting next after the filing of the
certificate or certificates mentioned in the preceding section, pay to the
engineer his additional fees therein mentioned, and shall, unless the
amount or amounts named in the said certificate or certificates including such additional fees, is forthwith paid by the respective parties
declared in said certificate or certificates to be liable to pay the same,
cause the amount or amounts and fees to be added to the collector's
roll, together with ten per cent. added thereto, and the same shall
thereupon become a charge against the lands of the party or parties so
liable, and shall be collected in the same manner as any other Municipal taxes, and when collected shall be paid over to the party or parties
entitled thereto.

16. All notices under the provisions of this Act, shall be served personally, or by leaving the same at the place of abode of the owner or
occupant, with a grown-up person residing thereat ; and in case of non-
residents, then upon the agent of the owner, or by registered letter
addressed to said owner at the post office nearest to his last known place
of abode.

17. Every Municipal Corporation shall have and exercise all the
rights and privileges of this Act, and may be made parties to the said
agreement or award, and shall be considered as owner of the highway
for the purposes of this Act, and shall in all respects be in the same
position as an individual owner.

18. In case any person during or after the construction of the ditch
or drain herein provided for, desires to avail himself of such ditch or
drain for the purpose of draining other lands than those contemplated
by the original proceedings, he may avail himself of the provisions of
this Act, as if he were or had been a party to such original proceedings ;
but no person shall make use of the ditch or drain constructed under
the provisions of this Act, unless under agreement or award pursuant
to its provisions as to the use of lands of others, as to the enlargement
of the original ditch or drain so as to contain additional water therein,
and as to the time for the completion of such enlargement.

19. Notwithstanding any of the lands through which the drain is required, are situate in a Municipality adjoining the one in which the original proceedings were commenced, the engineer shall have full power and authority to continue such ditch or drain in and through so much of the lands in such adjoining Municipality as may be found necessary, and all proceedings authorized under the provisions of this Act are to be had, taken, and carried on in the Municipality where commenced ; but in such case the Clerk of said Municipality shall forward to the Clerk of such adjoining Municipality a certified copy of the award, as made, confirmed, or altered, and shall also forward to him a certified copy of every certificate of the engineer which affects or relates to the lands in such adjoining Municipality, and to the owners thereof ; and such Muncipal Council shall, unless the amounts are forthwith paid by the parties declared by said certificate liable to pay the same, have and take all proceedings for the collection of the sums so certified to be paid, as though all the proceedings had been taken and carried on in such adjoining Municipality.

20. The fees to which the engineer shall be entitled under this Act shall be such as shall be fixed by By-law or resolution of the Council ; and in case no such fees are fixed by the Council the same shall be his legally authorized fees for similar work, or such less amount as may be agreed upon ; and the fees to witnesses and for the service of papers authorized by the Division Court Clerk, shall be the same as those allowed to witnesses, and similar services in the Division Court.

21. The word " engineer " in this Act shall mean civil engineer, land surveyor, or such person as the Municipality by By-law may deem competent to perform the duties required under this Act.

22. Chapter one hundred and ninety-nine of the Revised Statutes of Ontario, chapter twelve of the Acts passed in the forty-first year of the reign of Her Majesty, and chapter thirty of the Acts passed in the forty-third year of the reign of Her Majesty, are hereby repealed ; but all works commenced, and all proceedings had and taken thereunder, may be continued to completion as though this Act had not been passed.

FORM A.

Township of

Whereas it is found necessary that a ditch or drain should be made (deepened, or widened) on Lot No.   in the   concession of the Township of   and it is necessary to continue the same through lot number   in the   .·   concession of the township of   (*if more than one lot describe them*).

Therefore we   owners of the land hereinafter described, do agree each with the other as follows :—

That I,   owner of   (*describe lot*)   agree that I will make (deepen or widen) and maintain that part of such ditch or drain commencing at stake number one planted (*describing the locality of said stake*) and thence to stake number two, and that said portion of said ditch or drain shall be (*describing depth and width*, and I   owner of (*giving the name of each person, the land owned by him, the portion of work assigned, its depth, width, etc.*), and each of us agrees to have our said respective portions completed on or before the   ˙   day of   A.D. 18

Dated,   } (Signed by the Parties.)
Witness.   }

FORM B.

Township of

To

Sir,—As the owner of lot number   in the   concession
of the Township of   I require to construct a ditch or drain
through said lot, and find it necessary to continue the same through your
land, being lot number   in the   concession of the Township of   under the Ditches and Watercourses Act, 1883, and
request that you will attend at   on   the   day
of   18   at the hour of   o'clock, in the   noon,
with the object of agreeing, if possible, upon the respective portion of such
ditch or drain to be made, deepened or widened by the several parties interested.

Dated this   day of   18

Yours, &c.

———

FORM C.

To

Clerk of the municipality of the   of
Sir,—As the owner of lot number   in the   concession
of the Township of   I require to construct a ditch or drain through
said lot, and it will be necessary to continue the ditch or drain through the
following lands on lot number   in the   concession of the
Township of   owned by   , Lot number   in the
concession of the Township of   owned by   (*describe each
lot through which the ditch or drain must be continued, and the name of the owner
of each parcel*), and having failed to agree upon the respective portions to be
made by each, I (*or we*) require the engineer appointed by the Municipality
for the purpose, to attend at the locality of said proposed ditch or drain on
the   day of   18   at the hour of   o'clock in
the   noon, examine the premises, hear the parties and their witnesses, and make his award under the provisions of the Ditches and Water-
courses Act, 1883.

Dated   ~

(Signed by Party or Parties.)

———

FORM D.

To

Take notice that the engineer appointed by the Municipality for the
purpose will attend at lot number   in the   concession
of   on   the   day of   A.D. 18   at the
hour of   o'clock in the   noon, to examine the site of the
proposed ditch or drain and make his award therein ; and you as the owner
of (*describe the lot*) which may be affected thereby, are requested to attend
(with any witnesses you may desire to have heard) at said time and place.

Dated

Yours, &c.

FORM E.

I   the engineer appointed by the Municipality of the Township of   in the County of   under the provisions of the Ditches and Watercourses Act, 1883, having by the requisition of owner (or owners) of lot number   in the concession of the Township of   filed with the clerk of the said municipality, representing that he (or they) required a ditch or drain on said lot, and that it would be necessary to continue the ditch or drain through the following lands on lot number in the   concession of the Township of   owned by   etc., did attend at the time and place named in said notice, and having examined the locality of said ditch or drain, and heard the parties and their witnesses (if any), find and award as follows :—

That   lot number   in the concession of the Township of   would be benefitted by, and requires a ditch or drain (or the deepening or widening of a ditch or drain, if already made), to enable the proper cultivation or use of the said land, and I find that said ditch or drain will require to be extended across the land of   being lot number   in the concession of   and across the land of being   lot number   in the   concession of the Township of   (and so on, giving the name of each owner and lot to termination of said ditch or drain), and I award the making of said ditch or drain (or the deepening or widening as the case may be), as follows :— .... .shall commence at stake number one planted (describe with reasonable certainty where planted), and shall open up and maintain a ditch or drain (describe width and depth), to stake number two planted (describe where planted, distance and direction from first stake), and said portion shall be made and completed within (name time within which to be completed). That   shall commence at stake number two, above described, and shall open up and maintain a ditch or drain (describe width and depth) to stake number three planted (describe where planted, distance and direction from stake number two), and said portion shall be made and completed within (name time, etc.) That   shall, etc., (and so on to the termination of said ditch or drain).

. That my costs attendant upon the examination, and making of this award are   and shall be borne and paid as follows : (give the name of the persons to be charged therewith, and the portion to be borne by each).

Dated this   day of   A.D. 18

Witness.   } (Signature of Engineer.)

FORM F.

To   Clerk of the Township of   I hereby certify that   has completed certain work which under my award dated the   day of A.D. 18 , one   was ordered and adjudged to perform, and which the said   having failed to do was by me subsequently let to the said   for the sum of $ and the said   is entitled to be paid the said amount.

I further certify that my additional fees are   and that
said amount and said fees are   and that said amount and
said fees are chargeable on (*describe property to be charged therewith*)
and shall unless forthwith paid be added to the Collectrrs' Roll
(*with interest*) as provided in the fifteenth section of the Act respecting
Ditches and Watercourses, 1883.

Dated this   day of   A.D. 18

_____

Engineer for

_____

CHAPTER 198.—REVISED STATUTES OF ONTARIO.

AN ACT RESPECTING LINE FENCES.

Her Majesty, by and with the advice and consent of the Legislative
Assembly of the Province of Ontario, enacts as follows :

1. This Act may be cited as "*The Line Fences Act.*"

2. Owners of occupied adjoining lands shall make, keep up and
repair a just proportion of the fence which marks the boundary between
them, or if there is no fence, they shall so make, keep up and repair
the same proportion, which is to mark such boundary ; and owners of
unoccupied lands which adjoin occupied lands, shall, upon their being
occupied, be liable to the duty of keeping up and repairing such
proportion, and in that respect shall be in the same position as if their
land had been occupied at the time of the original fencing, and shall
be liable to the compulsory proceedings hereinafter mentioned.   37 V.
c. 25, s. 2.

3. In case of dispute between owners respecting such proportion,
the following proceedings shall be adopted :

(1.) Either owner may notify (Form 1)the other owner or the occupant
of the land of the owner so to be notified, that he will, not less than
one week from the service of such notice, cause three Fence-viewers
of the locality to arbitrate in the premises.

(2.) Such owners so notifying shall also notify (Form 2) the Fence-
viewers, not less than one week before their services are required.

(3.) The notices in both cases shall be in writing, signed by the person
notifying, and shall specify the time and place of meeting for the
arbitration, and may be served by leaving the same at the place of
abode of such owner or occupant, with some grown-up person residing
thereat ; or in case of such lands being untenanted, by leaving such
notice with any agent of such owner.

(4.) The owners notified may, within the week, object to any or all of
the Fence-viewers notified, and in case of disagreement, the Judge
hereinafter mentioned shall name the Fence-viewers who are to
arbitrate.   37 V. c. 25, s. 3.

4. An occupant, not the owner of land notified in the manner above
mentioned, shall immediately notify the owner ; and if he neglects so
to do, shall be liable for all damage caused to the owner by such
neglect.   37 V. c. 25, s. 9.

5. The Fence-viewers shall examine the premises, and if required by either party, they shall hear evidence, and are authorized to examine the parties and their witnesses on oath, any one of them may administer an oath or affirmation as in Courts of Law.   37 V. c. 25, s. 4.

6. The Fence-viewers shall make an award (Form 3) in writing signed by any two of them, respecting the matters so in dispute ; which award shall specify the locality, quantity, description and the lowest price of the fence it orders to be made, and the time within which the work shall be done, and shall state by which of the said parties the costs of the proceedings shall be paid, or whether either party shall pay some proportion of such costs.

(2.) In making such award, the Fence-viewers shall regard the nature of the fences in use in the locality, the pecuniary circumstances of the persons between whom they arbitrate, and generally the suitableness of the fence ordered to the wants of each party.

(3.) Where, from the formation of the ground, by reason of streams or other causes, it is found impossible to locate the fence upon the line between the parties, it shall be lawful for the Fence-viewers to locate the said fence either wholly or partially on the land of either of the said parties, where to them it seems to be most convenient ; but such location shall not in any way affect the title to the land.

(4.) If necessary, the Fence-viewers may employ a Provincial Land Surveyor, and have the locality described by metes and bounds.   37 V. c. 25, s. 5.

7. The award shall be deposited in the office of the Clerk of the Council of the Municipality in which the lands are situate, and shall be an official document, and may be given in evidence in any legal proceeding by certified copy, as are other official documents ; and notice of its being made shall be given to all parties interested.   37 V. c. 25, s. 6.

8. The award may be enforced as follows :—The person desiring to enforce it shall serve upon the owner or occupant of the adjoining lands a notice in writing, requiring him to obey the award, and if the award is not obeyed within one month after service of such notice, the person so desiring to enforce it may do the work which the award directs, and may immediately recover its value and the costs from the owner by action in any Division Court having jurisdiction in the locality : but the Judge of such Division Court may, on application of either party, extend the time for making such fence to such time as he may think just.   37 V. c. 25, s. 7.

9. The award shall constitute a lien and charge upon the lands respecting which it is made, when it is registered in the Registry Office of the County, or other Registration Division in which the lands are.

(2.) Such registration may be in duplicate or by copy, proved by affidavit of a witness to the original, or otherwise, as in the case of any deed which is within the meaning of " The Registry Act."   37 V. c. 25, s. 8.

10. The Fence-viewers shall be entitled to receive two dollars each for every day's work under this Act.   Provincial Land Surveyors and witnesses shall be entitled to the same compensation as if they were subpœnaed in any Division Court.   37 V. c. 25, s. 10.

11. Any person dissatisfied with the award made may appeal therefrom to the Judge of the County Court of the County in which the lands are situate, and the proceedings on such appeal shall be as follows .

(1.) The appellant shall serve upon the Fence-viewers, and all parties interested, a notice in writing of his intention to appeal within one week from the time he has been notified of the award ; which notice may be served as other notices mentioned in this Act.

(2.) The appellant shall also deliver a copy of such notice to the Clerk of the Division Court of the Division in which the land lies, and the Clerk shall immediately notify the Judge of such appeal, whereupon the Judge shall appoint a time for the hearing thereof, and, if he thinks fit, order such sum of money to be paid by the appellant to the said Clerk as will be sufficient indemnity against costs of the appeal.

(3.) The Judge shall order the time and place for the hearing of the appeal, and communicate the same to the Clerk, who shall notify the Fence-viewers and all parties interested, in the manner hereinbefore provided for the service of other notices under this Act.

(4.) The Judge shall hear and determine the appeal, and set aside, alter, or affirm the award, correcting any error therein, and he may examine parties and witnesses on oath, and, if he so pleases, may inspect the premises ; and may order payment of costs by either party, and fix the amount of such costs.

(5.) His decision shall be final ; and the award, as so altered or confirmed, shall be dealt with in all respects as it would have been if it had not been appealed from.

(6.) The practice and proceedings on the appeal, including the fees payable for subpœnas and the conduct money of witnesses, shall be the same, as nearly as may be, as in the case of a suit in the Division Court. 37 V. c. 25, s. 11 ; 40 V. c. 7, *Sched.* A. (202) ; 40 V. c. 8, s. 58.

12. Any agreement in writing (Form 4) between owners respecting such line fence may be filed or registered and enforced as if it was an award of Fence-viewers. 37 V. c. 25, s. 12.

13. The owner of the whole or part of a division or line fence which forms part of the fence enclosing the occupied or improved land of another person, shall not take down or remove any part of such fence,

(*a*) Without giving at least six months previous notice of his intention to the owner or occupier of such adjacent enclosure ;

(*b*) Nor unless such last mentioned owner or occupier after demand made upon him in writing by the owner of such fence, refuses to pay therefor the sum, to be determined as provided in the sixth section of this Act ;

(*c*) Nor if such owner or occupier will pay to the owner of such fence or of any part thereof, such sum as the Fence-viewers may award to be paid therefor under the sixth section of this Act. 40 V. c. 29, s. 1.

(2.) The provisions of this Act relating to the mode of determining disputes between the owner of occupied adjoining lands ; the manner of enforcing awards and appeals therefrom ; and the schedules of forms attached hereto, and all other provisions of this Act, so far as applicable, shall apply to proceedings under this section. 40 V. c. 29, s. 2.

14. If any tree is thrown down, by accident or otherwise, across a line or division fence, or in any way in and upon the property adjoining that upon which such tree stood, thereby causing damage to the crop upon such property or to such fence, it shall be the duty of the proprietor or occupant of the premises on which such tree theretofore stood, to remove the same forthwith, and also forthwith to repair the fence, and otherwise to make good any damage caused by the falling of such tree.

(2.) On his neglect or refusal so to do for forty-eight hours after notice in writing to remove the same, the injured party may remove the same, or cause the same to be removed, in the most convenient and inexpensive manner, and may make good the fence so damaged, and may retain such tree to remunerate him for such removal, and may also recover any further amount of damages beyond the value of such tree from the party liable to pay it under this Act.

(3.) For the purpose of such removal the owner of such tree may enter into and upon such adjoining premises for the removal of the same without being a trespasser, avoiding any unnecessary spoil or waste in so doing.

(4.) All disputes arising between parties relative to this section, and for the collection and recovery of all or any sums of money becoming due thereunder, shall be adjusted by three Fence-viewers of the Municipality, two of whom shall agree. 29-30 V. c. 51, s. 355 (28).

15. The forms in the Schedule hereto are to guide the parties, being varied according to circumstances. 37 V. c. 25, s. 13.

SCHEDULE OF FORMS.
FORM 1.
(*Section* 3.)
NOTICE TO OPPOSITE PARTY.

Take notice, that Mr. , Mr. , and Mr. , three fence-viewers of this locality, will attend on the day of , 18 , at the hour of , to view and arbitrate upon the line fence in dispute between our properties, being Lots (*or* parts of Lots) *One* and *Two* in the Concession of the Township of . , in the County of , .

Dated this day of , 18 .

A. B.,
Owner of Lot 1.

To C. D.,
Owner of Lot 2.

FORM 2.
(*Section* 3.)
NOTICE TO FENCE-VIEWERS.

Take notice, that I require you to attend at on the day of , A.D. 18 , at o'clock A.M., to view and arbitrate on the line fence between my property and that of Mr. , being Lots (*or* parts of Lots) Nos. *One* and *Two* in the Concession of the Township of , in the County of

Dated this day of , 18 .

A. B.,
Owner of Lot 1.

FORM 3.

(*Section* 6.)

AWARD.

We, the fence-viewers of (*name of the locality*), having been nominated to view and arbitrate upon the line fence between   by (*name and description of owner who notified*) and (*name and description of owner notified*), which fence is to be made and maintained between (*describe properties*), and having examined the premises and duly acted according to "*The Line Fences Act*," do award as follows : That part of the said line which commences at   and ends at   (*describe the points*) shall be fenced, and the fence maintained by the said   , and that part thereof which commences at   and ends at   (*describe the points*) shall be fenced, and the fence maintained by the said   .
The fence shall be of the following description (*state the kind of fence, height, material, &c.*), and shall cost at least   per rod. The work shall be commenced within   days, and completed within   days from this date, and the costs shall be paid by (*state by whom paid ; if by both, in what proportion*).

Dated this   day of   , A.D. 18 .

                                        ` *Signatures of fence-viewers.*)

FORM 4.

(*Section* 12.)

AGREEMENT.

We   and   , owners respectively of Lots (*or parts of Lots*) *One* and *Two* in the   Concession of the Township of   , in the County of   , do agree that the line fence which divides our said properties shall be made and maintained by us as follows : (*follow the same form as award.*)

Dated this   ●day of   , A.D. 18 .

                                        (*Signatures of parties.*)

CHAPTER 10.

An Act to amend the Line Fences Act.

[ASSENTED TO 7TH MARCH, 1878.]

Her Majesty, by and with the advice and consent of the Legislative Assembly of the Province of Ontario, enacts as follows :

1. In the Line Fences Act, being chapter one hundred and ninety-eight of the Revised Statutes of Ontario, the expression "occupied lands," shall not include so much of a lot, parcel or farm as is unenclosed, although a part of such lot, parcel or farm is enclosed and in actual use and occupation.

CHAPTER 42.

An Act to further amend the Line Fences Act.

[ASSENTED TO 25TH MARCH, 1884.]

Her Majesty, by and with the advice and consent of the Legislative Assembly of the Province of Ontario, enacts as follows :

1. Where, within the meaning of section 3 of " *The Line Fences Act,*" there is any dispute between owners or occupants of lands situate in different municipalities, the following words or expressions in said Act shall have the meaning hereinafter expressed, namely :

(1.) The phrase "fence-viewers" shall mean two fence-viewers of the municipality in which is situate the land of the owner or occupant notified under sub-section 1 of section 3 of said Act, and one fence-viewer of the municipality in which is situate the land of the party or person giving the notice ; except that in case of a disagreement having occurred within the meaning of sub-section 4 of said section, the said phrase "fence-viewers" shall mean fence-viewers from either or both municipalities.

(2.) The expression "in which the lands are situate" and the expression "in which the land lies," shall respectively mean "in which are situate the lands of the owner or occupant so notified under said sub-section one."

CHAPTER 37.

An Act to prevent the spread of Noxious Weeds, and of Diseases affecting Fruit Trees.

[ASSENTED TO 25TH MARCH, 1884.]

Her Majesty, by and with the advice and consent of the Legislative Assembly of the Province of Ontario, enacts as follows :

1. Chapter 188 of the Revised Statues of Ontario, entitled "*An Act to prevent the spreading of Canada Thistles,*" chapter 33 of the Acts passed in the forty-second year of Her Majesty's reign, entitled "*An Act to protect Plum and Cherry Trees,*" and chapter 28 of the Acts passed in the forty-fourth year of Her Majesty's reign, entitled "*An Act to prevent the spread of the Yellows among Peach, Nectarine and other Trees,*" are hereby repealed.

2. It shall be the duty of every owner of land, or the occupant thereof if the owner is not resident within the local municipality wherein the same is situate—(1) To cut down or destroy all the Canada thistles, ox-eye daisy, wild oats, rag-weed and burdock growing on his land, and all other noxious weeds growing on his land to which this Act may be extended by by-law of the municipality, so often each and • every year as is sufficient to prevent the ripening of their seed ; (2) To cut out and burn all the black-knot found on plum or cherry trees on his land, so often each and every year as it shall appear on such trees ; and (3) To cut down and burn any peach, nectarine or other trees on his land infected with the disease known as the yellows, and to destroy all the fruit of trees so infected

3. (1) The Council of any city, town, township or incorporated village may by by-law extend the operation of this Act to any other weed or weeds or to any other disease of fruit trees or fruit which they declare to be noxious to husbandry or gardening in the municipality ; and all the provisions of this Act shall apply to such noxious weeds and diseases as if the same were herein enumerated.

(2) Any such Council may, and upon a petition of fifty or more ratepayers shall appoint at least one Inspector to enforce the provisions of this Act in the municipality, and fix the amount of remuneration, fees or charges he is to receive for the performance of his duties ; and in case a vacancy shall occur in the office of Inspector, it shall be the duty of the Council to fill the same forthwith.

(3) The Council of any township in which there are any large tracts or blocks of waste or unoccupied land, may upon the petition of not less than thirty ratepayers, by by-law suspend the operation of this Act, in respect of such waste or unoccupied lands ; the by-law to define with sufficient clearness the tracts or blocks of land so exempted ; such by-law to remain in force until repealed by such Council ; and until repealed the lands therein described shall be exempt from the operation of this Act.

4. (1) It shall be the duty of such Inspector to give or cause to be given notice in writing to the owner or occupant of any land within the municipality whereon the said noxious weeds are growing and in danger of going to seed (and in case of property of a railway company, such notice shall be given to any station-master of such company resident in or nearest to the municipality), requiring him to cause the same to be cut down or destroyed within ten days from the service of such notice ; and it shall be the duty of the Inspector to give or cause to be given such notice for the first time not later than the tenth day of July in each year, or such other earlier date as may be fixed by by-law of the municipality.

(2) In case such owner or occupant of land (or, if it be railway property, then the station-master upon whom notice has been served) refuses or neglects to cut down or destroy all or any of the said noxious weeds within the period aforesaid, the said Inspector shall enter upon the land and cause such weeds to be cut down or destroyed with as little damage to growing crops as may be, and he shall not be liable to be sued in action of trespass therefor ; or the Inspector, instead of entering upon the land and causing such weeds to be cut down or destroyed, may lay information before any Justice of the Peace as to such refusal or neglect, and such owner or occupant shall, upon conviction, be liable to the penalties imposed by section 10 of this Act.

(3) But no such Inspector shall have power to cut down or destroy noxious weeds on any land sown with grain ; and where such noxious weeds are growing upon non-resident lands it shall not be necessary to give any notice before proceeding to cut down or destroy the same.

5. (1) The said Inspector shall keep an accurate account of the expense incurred by him in carrying out the provisions of the preceding sections of this Act with respect to each parcel of land entered upon therefor, and shall deliver a statement, of such expenses, describing the land entered upon, and verified by oath, to the owner or occupant of resident lands, requiring him to pay the amount.

(2) If any owner or occupant of land amenable under the provisions of this Act deems such expense excessive, an appeal may be had to the said Council (if made within thirty days after the delivery of such statement), and the said Council shall determine the matter in dispute.

(3) In case the owner or occupant of resident lands refuses or neglects to pay the same within thirty days after such request for payment, the said claim shall be presented to the Council of the municipality in which such expense was incurred, and the said Council is hereby authorized and required to audit and allow such claim, and order the same to be paid from the fund for general purposes of the said municipality.

6. The said Inspector shall also present to the said Council a similar statement, verified by oath, of the expenses incurred by him in carrying out the provisions of this Act upon any non-resident lands; and the said Council is hereby authorized and required to audit and allow the same, or so much thereof as to said Council may seem just, and to pay so much thereof as has been so allowed.

7. The Council of the municipality shall cause all such sums as have been so allowed and paid by the council under the provisions of this Act to be by the Clerk severally placed upon the collector's roll of the municipality against the lands described in the statement of the Inspector, and to be collected in the same manner as other taxes imposed by by-laws of the municipality.

8. It shall be the duty of the Overseers of highways in any municipality to see that the provisions of this Act relating to noxious weeds are carried out within their respective highway divisions, by cutting down or destroying or causing to be cut down or destroyed at the proper time to prevent the ripening of their seed, all the noxious weeds growing on the highways or road allowances within their respective divisions; such work to be performed as part of the ordinary statute labour, or to be paid for at a reasonable rate by the Treasurer of the municipality, as the Council of the municipality may direct.

9. If written complaint be made to the Inspector that yellows or black-knot exist within the municipality, in any locality described in such complaint with reasonable certainty, he shall proceed to examine the fruit trees in such locality, and if satisfied of the presence of either disease he shall immediately give notice in writing to the owner or occupant of the land whereon the affected trees are growing, requiring him within five days from the receipt of said notice to deal with such trees in the manner provided by section 2 of this Act.

10. (1) Any owner or occupant of land who refuses or neglects to cut down or destroy any of the said noxious weeds, after notice given by the Inspector, as provided by section 4, or who knowingly suffers any of the said noxious weeds to grow thereon, and the seed to ripen so as to cause or endanger the spread thereof, or who suffers any black-knot to remain on plum or cherry trees, or keeps any peach, nectarine or other trees infected with yellows or the fruit of trees so infected, shall upon conviction be liable to a fine of not less than five nor more than twenty dollars for every such offence.

(2) Any person who knowingly sells or offers to sell any grass, clover or other seed, or any seed grain among which there is seed of Canada thistles, ox-eye daisy, wild oats, rag-weed, burdock or wild mustard, shall, for every such offence, upon conviction, be liable to a fine of not less than five nor more than twenty dollars.

(3) Any person who knowingly offers for sale or shipment, or sells or ships the fruit of trees infected with yellows shall, upon conviction, be liable to a fine of not less than five nor more than twenty dollars.

(4) Every Inspector, Overseer of highways, or other officer, who refuses or neglects to discharge the duties imposed on him by this Act, shall, upon conviction, be liable to a fine of not less than ten nor more than twenty dollars.

11. Every offence against the provisions of this Act shall be punished, and the penalty imposed for each offence shall be recovered and levied, on summary conviction, before any Justice of the Peace ; and all fines imposed shall be paid to the Treasurer of the municipality in which the offence is committed, for the use of the municipality.

12. The Council of every municipality in Ontario shall require its Inspector, Overseer of highways and other officers to faithfully discharge all their duties under this Act.

13. Where used in this Act the term "non-resident land" shall apply to all lands which are unoccupied, and the owner of which is not resident within the municipality, and the term "resident lands" shall apply to all lands which are occupied or which are owned by persons resident within the municipality

---

SCHEDULE A.

Section 69.

BY-LAW IN FORCE IN EVERY MUNICIPALITY TILL ALTERED BY THE MUNICIPAL COUNCIL.

1. It shall be the duty of the Medical Health Officer to assist and advise the Board and its officers, in matters relating to public health, and to superintend, under the direction of the Board, the enforcement and observance, within this municipality, of Health By-laws or Regulations, and of Public Health Acts, and of any other Sanitary Laws, and, if thought advisable by the Board of School Trustees, to act as Medical Inspector of Schools, as well as advisory officer in matters pertaining to school hygiene, and to perform such other duties and lawful acts for the preservation of public health, as may, in his opinion, be necessary, or as may be required by the Board of Health. He shall also present to this Board, before the fifteenth day of November in each year, a full report upon the sanitary condition of the district.

2. The Sanitary Inspector, besides performing the duties hereafter indicated by this By-law as belonging specially to him, shall assist the Medical Health Officer, and perform such other duties as may from time to time be assigned to him by the Board of Health or its Chairman.

3. The Chairman of the Board of Health shall, before the first day of December in each year, present to the Municipal Council or Municipal Councils, comprised within his district, a report containing a detailed statement of the work of the Board during the year, and the report of the sanitary condition of the Municipality, as rendered to the Board by the Medical Health Officer. A copy of each such report shall be transmitted by the Secretary to the Secretary of the Provincial Board of Health.

4. No person shall within this municipality suffer the accumulation upon his premises, or deposit, or permit the deposit, upon any lot belonging to him, of anything which may endanger the public health, or deposit upon, on, or into, any street, square, lane, by-way, wharf, dock, slip, lake, pond, bank, harbor, river, stream, sewer, or water, any manure or other refuse, or vegetable or animal matter, or other filth.

5. It shall be the duty of the Sanitary Inspector, to keep a vigilant supervision over all streets, lanes, by-ways, lots, or premises, upon which any such accumulation as aforesaid may be found, and at once to notify the parties who own or occupy such lots or premises, or who either personally or through their employees, have deposited such manure, refuse, matter, dirt, or filth, in any street, lane, or by-way, to cleanse the same, and to remove what is found thereon ; such parties shall forthwith remove the same, and if the same be not removed within twenty-four hours after such notification, the Inspector may prosecute the parties so offending, and he may also cause the same to be removed at the expense of the person or persons so offending. He shall also inspect at intervals, as directed by the Board of Health, all premises occupied by persons residing within its jurisdiction, and shall report to the Board each and every case of violation of any of the provisions of this By-law, or of any other regulations for the preservation of the public health, and shall also report every case of refusal to permit him to make such inspection.

6. Whenever it shall appear to the Board, or to any of its officers, that it is necessary for the preservation of the public health, or for the abatement of anything dangerous to the public health, or whenever they or he shall have received a notice signed by one or more inhabitant householders of this municipality, stating the condition of any building in the municipality to be so filthy as to be dangerous to the public health, or that upon any premises in the municipality there is any foul or offensive ditch, gutter, drain, privy, cesspool, ashpit, or cellar, kept or constructed so as to be dangerous or injurious to the public health, or that upon any such premises an accumulation of dung, manure, offal, filth, refuse, stagnant water, or other matter, or thing, is kept so as to be dangerous or injurious as aforesaid, it shall be the duty of the Sanitary Inspector to enter such buildings or premises for the purpose of examining the same, and, if necessary, he shall order the removal of such matter or thing as aforesaid. If the occupant, or proprietor, or his lawful agent or representative, having charge or control of such premises, after having had twenty-four hours notice from any such officer of the Board of Health to remove or abate such matter or thing as aforesaid, shall neglect or refuse to remove or abate the same, he shall be subject to the penalties imposed under section 18 of this By-law.

.7. If the Board is satisfied upon due examination, that a cellar, room, tenament, or building within its jurisdiction, occupied as a dwelling-place, has become by reason of the number of occupants, want of cleanliness, the existence therein of a contagious or infectious disease, or other cause, unfit for such purpose, or that it has become a nuisance, or in any way dangerous to the health of the occupants, or of the public, they may issue a notice in writing to such occupants, or any of them, requiring the said premises to put in proper sanitary condition, or if they see fit, requiring the occupants to quit the premises within such time as the Board may deem reasonable. If the persons so notified, or any of them, neglect or refuse to comply with the terms of the notice, every person so offending shall be liable to the penalties imposed by section 18 of this By-law, and the Board may cause the premises to be properly cleaned at the expense of the owners or occupants, or may remove the occupants forcibly and close up the premises, and the same shall not again be occupied as a dwelling-place until put into proper sanitary condition.

8. No proprietor or tenant of any shop, house or outhouse, shall, nor shall any butcher or other person, use any such house, shop or outhouse at any time as a slaughter-house or for the purpose of slaughtering any animals therein, unless such shop, house or outhouse be distant not less than two hundred yards from any dwelling-house and distant not less than seventy yards from any public street.

9. All slaughter-houses within this municipality shall be subject to regular inspection under the direction of the Board of Health; and no person shall keep any slaughter-house unless the permission in writing of the Board for the keeping of such slaughter-house has been first obtained, and remains unrevoked. Such permission shall be granted, after approval of such premises upon inspection, subject to the condition that the said houses shall be so kept as not to impair the health of persons residing in their vicinity, and upon such condition being broken the said permission may be revoked by the Board; and all animals to be slaughtered, and all fresh meat exposed for sale in this municipality shall be subject to like inspection.

10. All milch cows and cow byres and all dairies or other places in which milk is sold or kept for general use, and all cheese factories and creameries shall be subject to regular inspection under the direction of the said Board; and the proprietors shall be required to obtain permission in writing from the Board, to keep such dairy or other place in which milk is sold or kept as aforesaid, or to keep a cheese factory or creamery, and the same shall not be kept by anyone without such permission, which shall be granted after approval of such premises upon inspection, subject to the condition that all such places as aforesaid are so kept and conducted that the milk shall not contain any matter or thing liable to produce disease either by reason of adulteration, contamination with sewage, absorption of disease germs, infection of cows, or any other generally recognized cause, and upon such condition being broken the said permission may be revoked by the Board.

11. No person shall offer for sale as food within this municipality any diseased animal, or any meat, fish, fruit, vegetables, milk, or other article of food which, by reason of disease, adulteration, impurity, or any other cause shall be unfit for use.

12. It shall be the duty of the owner of every house within this municipality to provide for the occupants of the same a sufficient supply of wholesome drinking water; and in case the occupant or occupants of any such house is or are not satisfied with the wholesomeness or sufficiency of such supply, he or they may apply to the Board of Health to determine as to the same; and if the supply be sufficient and wholesome, then the expenses incident to such determination shall be paid by the said occupant or occupants, and if not, then they shall be paid by the owner; and in either case the said charges shall be recoverable in the same manner as municipal taxes.

13. All wells in this municipality which are in use, whether such wells are public or private, shall be cleaned out before the 1st day of July in each year, and in case the Board of Health certifies that any well should be filled up, such well shall be forthwith filled up by the owner of the premises.

14. The following code of rules and regulations for the disposal of sewage and refuse shall constitute a part of this By-law, and any person or persons violating or neglecting any of the said rules and regulations shall be liable to the fines and penalties imposed by section 18 of this By-law.

Rule 1.—No privy-vault, cesspool or reservoir into which a privy, water-closet, stable or sink is drained, shall be established until the details of such establishment shall have been submitted to and obtained the approval in writing of the Medical Health Officer, who shall, from time to time, determine with the approbation of the Board, the method of disposal of excreta, sewage and other refuse, to be adopted within the district.

Rule 2.—Earth privies or earth closets without a vault below the surface of the ground do not come within Rule 1, but sufficient dry earth, wood-ashes or coal-ashes to absorb all the fluid parts of the deposit must be thrown upon the contents of such earth privies and closets daily, the contents when removed from the closet must be placed in a shed or box with rain-proof cover, and removed from the premises at least once a year on or before the fifteenth day of May.

RULE 3.—If the exigencies or circumstances of the municipality require that privy-vaults, cesspools or reservoirs shall be allowed in accordance with Rule 1, they shall be cleaned out at least once a year, on or before the fifteenth day of May, and from the fifteenth day of May to the first day of November in each year they shall be thoroughly disinfected by adding to the contents of the vault, cesspool or reservoir, once a month, not less than two pounds of sulphate of copper, dissolved in two pailfuls of water, or other suitable disinfectant.

RULE 4.—Within the limits of this municipality no night-soil or contents of any cesspool shall be removed unless previously deodorized as above, and during its transportation the material shall be covered with a layer of fresh earth, except the removal shall have been by some "Odorless Excavating Process."

RULE 5.—All putrid and decaying animal or vegetable matter must be removed from all cellars, buildings, out-buildings and yards on or before the fifteenth day of May in each year.

RULE 6.—Every householder and every hotel and restaurant-keeper or other person shall dispose of all garbage, for the disposal of which he is responsible, either by burning the same or by placing it in a proper covered receptacle for swill and house offal, the contents of which shall, between the fifteenth day of May and the first day of November, be regularly removed as often as twice a week.

RULE 7.—Between the fifteenth day of May and the first day of November, no hog shall be kept within the limits of this municipality, except in pens seventy feet from any house with floors kept free from standing water and regularly cleaned and disinfected.

RULE 8.—The keeper of every livery or other stable shall keep his stable and stable-yard clean, and shall not permit, between the fifteenth day of May and the first day of November, more than two waggon-loads of manure to accumulate in or near the same at any one time, except by permission of the Board of Health.

15. The following regulations regarding the construction of houses, shall be in force within this municipality :—

RULE 1.—No house shall be built in or upon any site, the soil of which has been made up of any refuse, unless such soil shall have been removed from such site, and the site disinfected, or unless the said soil shall have been covered with a layer of charcoal, covered by a layer of concrete at least six inches thick and of such additional thickness as may be requsite under the circumstances to prevent the escape of gases into such proposed house.

RULE 2.—The drain of every house which may be connected with a sewer or cesspool shall be ventilated by means of a pipe extending upward from the highest point of the main soil or waste-pipe, and also by a pipe carried upward from the drain outside the walls of the house according to the principles shown on diagram, page 143, Ont. Stat., 1884. These pipes shall be of the same dimensions as the said main soil or waste-pipe, and shall be constructed of the same material or of stout galvanized iron, and no trap shall intervene between the said ventilating pipes. In case a trap shall intervene between the sewer or cesspool, and the ventilating pipes already described, then a four-inch ventilating pipe of the same material as above described shall be carried from a point between such trap and the sewer All such ventilating pipes shall be carried above the roof of the said house, and shall open above at points sufficiently remote from every window, door, sky-light, chimney or other opening leading into any house.

No pipe carrying air or gas from any drain or soil-pipe shall be connected with any chimney in a dwelling-house, unless the same be a furnace chimney used exclusively for the purpose of ventilating such soil-pipe or drain.

RULE 3.—Every house-drain shall be constructed of vitrified earthenware or iron pipe ; and every soil and waste pipe, of iron pipe rendered impervious to gas or liquids, the joints thereof being run with lead and caulked, or of lead pipe weighing at least 6 lbs. to the square foot ; and the waste pipe from every closet, sink, tub, wash-basin, safe or other service shall have as near as may be to the point of junction with such service a trap so constructed, vented and furnished, that it shall at no time allow of the passage of gas into such house. All joints shall be so constructed as to prevent gas escaping through them.

RULE 4.—The construction of any closet or other convenience which shall allow of the escape into the house of air or gas which has been confined in any part of it or from the drain or soil pipe, is hereby prohibited.

RULE 5.—No refrigerator waste shall be allowed to connect with any drain.

RULE 6.—No pipe supplying water directly to a water-closet or urinal, shall be connected with the pipe supplying water for drinking purposes.

16. Every person who erects, or causes to be erected, any building shall, within two weeks of the completion thereof, deposit in the Registry Office of the Registry Division in which the building is situated, plans of the drainage and plumbing of the same as executed ; and in the case of any alteration of any such plumbing or drainage, it shall be the duty of the owner of the house, within two weeks of the making of the alteration, to deposit in the same manner the plan and record of any such alteration ; if such alteration is made by a tenant, it shall be the duty of the tenant or lessee to deposit or cause to be deposited the plan and record of such alteration.

17. The following rules for preventing the spread of infectious and contagious diseases shall constitute a part of this By-law :—

RULE 1.—The Medical Health Officer [or Secretary of the Local Board of Health] shall provide each medical practitioner, practising within this municipality, with blank forms on which to report to the said Medical Health Officer [or Secretary] any case of diphtheria, small-pox, scarlet fever, cholera, typhoid fever, measles, whooping-cough or other disease dangerous to the public health ; and, also, with other blank forms on which to report death or recovery from any such disease.

RULE 2.—All such forms shall be so printed, gummed and folded that they may be readily sealed, without the use of an envelope, so as to keep them from perusal until opened by the Medical Health Officer [or Secretary.]

RULE 3.—Said blanks shall be in accordance with the following forms :—

Report of Infectious Disease.

Christian name and surname of patient :
Age of patient :

Locality, (giving street, number of house or lot), where patient is :
Name of disease :
Name of school attended by children from that house :
Measures employed for isolation and disinfection :

(Signature of physician) :

....

Report of Death or Recovery from Infectious Disease.

Christian name and surname of patient :
Locality, (giving street, number of house or lot), where patient is :
Name of disease :

How long sick :
Whether dead or recovered
Means of disinfection employed, and when employed :
(Signature of physician) :
....

RULE 4.—The Medical Health Officer [or Secretary], within six hours after he shall have received a notice of the existence of scarlet fever, diphtheria, small-pox, cholera, or whooping-cough, in any house, shall affix or cause to be affixed by the head of the household, or by some other person, near the entrance of such house a card at least nine inches wide and twelve inches long, stating that such disease exists in the said house, and stating the penalty for removal of such card without the permission of the Medical Health Officer or Board of Health.

RULE 5.—No person shall remove such card without the permission of the Board of Health or one of its officers.

RULE 6.—No animal affected with an infectious or contagious disease shall be brought or kept within this municipality, except by permission of the Board of Health.

18. Any person who violates section 4, 6, 7, 9 or 11 of this by-law, or Rule 1 of section 15, or Rule 5 or 6 of section 17, shall be liable for every such offence to a penalty of not less than $5 nor more than $50 in the discretion of the convicting Justices or Magistrate, besides costs, which may also be inflicted if the committing Justices or Magistrate see fit to impose the same. Any person who violates any other provision of this By-law shall be liable for every such offence to a penalty not exceeding $20, in the discretion of the convicting Justices or Magistrate, besides costs, which may also be inflicted if the convicting Justices or Magistrate see fit to impose the same. Every such penalty may be recovered by any person before any two Justices or a Police Magistrate having jurisdiction in the municipality, and shall be levied by distress and sale of the goods and chattels of the offender, with the costs of such distress and sale, by warrant under the hands and seals of the Justices, or the hand and seal of the Police Magistrate, before whom the same are recovered, or under the hands and seals of any other two Justices having jurisdiction in the municipality, and in default of sufficient distress the said Justices or Magistrate may commit the offender to the Common Gaol or to any Lockup or House of Correction in the said municipality for any time not exceeding fourteen days, with or without hard labor, unless the amount imposed be sooner paid.

SCHEDULE B.

FORM OF MUNICIPAL BY-LAW AMENDING THE ABOVE BY-LAW.

By-law Number —, intituled " A By-law respecting the Public Health By-law.

Whereas it is expedient to amend or repeal some of the provisions of the By-law appended to *The Public Health Act*, 1884, so far as the same are in force in this municipality, and to suspend the operation of other provisions of the said By-law.
Be it therefore enacted by the Municipal Council of
1. Section 13 of the said By-law is hereby amended by substituting the "first day of July of every second year" for "the first day of July in each year."
2. Rule 7 of section 14 of the said by-law is amended by striking out the words "and disinfected" at the end of the said rule.
3. Rule 2 of Section 15 shall not be in force in this municipality until the First day of January 1885.
4. Rule 3 of section 14 is hereby repealed.
5. This By-law shall go into force forthwith.

www.ingramcontent.com/pod-product-compliance
Lightning Source LLC
Chambersburg PA
CBHW022018190326
41519CB00010B/1555

*9 7 8 3 7 4 1 1 8 4 4 0 6 *